LOBBYING
IN
AMERICAN
POLITICS

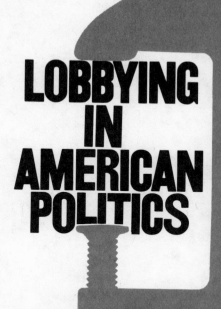

LOBBYING IN AMERICAN POLITICS

FRED J. COOK

FRANKLIN WATTS   NEW YORK   LONDON   1976

Library of Congress Cataloging in Publication Data

Cook, Fred J
  Lobbying in American politics.

  Bibliography: p.
  Includes index.
  SUMMARY: Discusses, through case studies, the development of lobbying as force in American politics and the
methods used by lobbyists to exert pressure on the
government.
  1. Lobbying—the United States—Case studies—Juvenile
literature. 2. Lobbyists—United States—Case studies—Juvenile literature. [1. Lobbying. 2. Politics, Practical] I. Title.
JK1118.C63   329′.03′0973   75-34286
ISBN 0-531-01143-7

CONTENTS

LOBBYING
IN
AMERICAN
POLITICS

Arthur H. Samish deserves a special niche in the story of the American political process as the unsurpassed prototype of the influence-wielders known as lobbyists. Samish never ran for public office, never held any important official position, and remained for decades largely unknown to the great mass of the people of California. Yet during those same decades he was in effect the uncrowned king of what was soon to become the most populous state in the nation.

Never a man to parade down the aisle in any modesty sweepstakes, Samish became so powerful and so immune that he could not resist the temptation to brag about his power. Brash and uninhibited, he produced for incredulous reporters some of the most outrageous quotes ever to drop from the lips of one of those ubiquitous shadow men who, from the earliest days of the republic, have worked secretively behind the scenes to advance the interests of themselves and their clients.

"I am the governor of the legislature," Samish proclaimed on one occasion. "To hell with the governor of California."

When Lester Velie of *Collier's* magazine interviewed him in 1949, Samish rattled off one hair-raising quote after another. He told Velie he ran "the damnedest Gestapo you ever saw," that he kept the findings of his secret agents in fat black books locked in his safe, and that from these dossiers he could tell "if a man wants a baked potato, a girl or money."

Warming up for his own exposé, Samish had a sudden inspiration. Velie's photographer was snapping some pictures,

THE UNCROWNED KING

ınd Samish interrupted: "You want the real picture? I'll give you some-
:hing that tells the whole story."

He produced a ventriloquist's dummy, a hobo with a circus
clown's grin, white gloves, and top hat. Perching the dummy on his lap,
Samish told the dumbfounded Velie and photographer, "That's the
way I lobby. That's my legislature. That's Mr. Legislature. 'How are you
today, Mr. Legislature?' "

The picture and the quotes were soon to produce a sensation
across the land, but Samish still had a topper. Before the stunned Velie
could catch his breath, the uncrowned king of California had another
and even more outrageous thought.

"If you can get a ladder long enough and put it against the
Capitol dome," he said, "you can get a picture of me unscrewing the
gold cupola."

As might have been expected, when *Collier's* sent these remarks
ricocheting across the nation even the uncrowned king discovered that
he had bought a peck of trouble. Senator Estes Kefauver was about to
launch the cross-continent, crime-busting crusade that was to make him
famous, and the outspoken Samish had elected himself a witness for the
Kefauver caravan when it reached California.

Kefauver, who had a field day questioning Mafia thugs and
crime-corrupted politicians, found Samish a far more suave and slippery
customer. The crime-prober and the lobbyist sparred for several rounds,
but hardly laid a glove on each other. Afterward, Kefauver, evidently
amazed at the flawed human gem he had discovered, felt impelled to
outdo Samish in verbal virtuosity. And so he gave this description of the
uncrowned king of California:

"In both personality and physique, Samish is a remarkable
figure. Physically, he stands over six feet, two inches in height, and must
weigh better than three hundred pounds. He is bald with a monk's
tonsure of gray fringe, and his face has the bland innocence of the
enfant terrible about to light a firecracker under his nurse's chair. In
manner, he is a combination of Falstaff, Little Boy Blue and Machia-
velli, crossed with an eel."

It would be impossible to improve on that description of the
supreme lobbyist or to find a better introduction to a discussion of the
checkered profession that in the course of American history has worked
for both good and evil.

★

The dictionary defines the verb "to lobby" this way: "to address or solicit members of a legislative body in the lobby or elsewhere, with intent to influence legislation." It has often been pointed out that such lobbying is a right guaranteed by the First Amendment to the Constitution, which protects, not only free speech and a free press, but "the right of the people ... to petition the Government for a redress of grievances."

Average Americans write or wire public officials, expressing their views on the issues of the day, but such individual communications have slight impact compared to the influence wielded by organized lobbying. That is conducted in the halls of Congress or the state capitols by specialists, often skilled lawyers or highly paid public relations men heavily financed by some special-interest group and relying on personal contacts with government officials. The disparity in opportunity and influence is obvious.

Former President Harry S. Truman, during a television interview with Edward R. Murrow in 1958, estimated that about 15 million Americans were represented by professional lobbies—but 150 million were not. As Truman saw it, only the President could protect those who had no lobby working for them, and if the President didn't do the job, the great bulk of the American people would be in deep trouble.

This was exactly the situation during the decades that witnessed the transformation of America from an agrarian to an industrial society. Powerful interests corrupted state and national governments on a vast scale, giving the profession of lobbying an unsavory reputation. Karl Schriftgiesser, who had intimate knowledge of the Washington scene from long service with congressional committees, described the post-Civil War period in these words:

"Most of the big industrial interests, however ruthless with each other they may have been in scrambling for the hog's share of the profits, found common ground in their opposition to labor unions, agriculture, and governmental regulations and controls. . . . Each lobby, working away in Washington, had but one end: to make government amenable to the measures it advocated; but all of them, working in coalition, were struggling to capture the government itself. By 1924 the big business, industrial and financial pressure groups had all but succeeded in their aims. After 1932 they were momentarily checked."

The mass of legislation introduced in Congress each new session is so stupendous that it overwhelms congressional staffs, who find it

impossible to become fully and independently informed about everything. In this situation, lobbyists become helpful. Representative
Richard Bolling (Democrat, Missouri) has called lobbies "indispens-
able" to the functioning of government. He argues that a conscientious
congressman can get a wealth of information from opposing lobbyists
who present him with both sides of an issue. On labor legislation, for instance, the mighty AFL-CIO lobby will be active on one side while the
immensely powerful U.S. Chamber of Commerce and National Association of Manufacturers will present opposing arguments. "The fair-
minded lobbyist will often state his position, and then candidly inform
the Member of what the opposition's argument is," Bolling writes.

As such a brief survey indicates, lobbyists in the past have generally represented special interests intent on prying extra benefits from
the government at the expense of the general public—those millions of
Americans about whom President Truman worried. It is only within the
last decade that broad-based people's lobbies have acquired the muscle
and resources to match those of the special interests. Such lobbies now
work actively on environmental issues, highway safety, public health,
and the reform of government itself.

This movement may be said to have begun with Ralph Nader,
and it has been taken up by John Gardner, the head of Common Cause.
Together, these men and their organizations are building "people's
lobbies" on a scale and with an influence unmatched in American
history. Their activities hold out the best hope of curbing the machi-
nations of the most traditional special-interest lobbyists—men like
Arthur H. Samish, who devoted his not inconsiderable talents to the
task of saving his clients vast sums of money.

Samish was born in San Francisco on August 9, 1897. His father
decamped when Samish was about three years old, and the boy was
reared by his mother, "a fine, gentle woman" who devoted her life to
him. When San Francisco was devastated by earthquake and fire on
April 18, 1906, the Samish family was burned out and had to subsist for
a time on food obtained from a relief station.

They finally secured new living quarters on the outskirts of the
city. There Samish's mother ran a boardinghouse, and the boy peddled
newspapers, ran errands, and did odd jobs to eke out the family income.
He was a hustler, ever active, with little love for school. As he later told
Bob Thomas, the California journalist who wrote his story: "I was in
and out of grammar schools all over town. Mostly out. I was a hell raiser

even then—I liked playing handball and having fun instead of study-ing." His grades were poor, he was constantly in trouble with his teachers, and in the seventh grade he quit.

In the next years he worked at a variety of jobs. He grew tall and strong, standing some six feet two by the time he was sixteen. He loved a good time, fancied himself as a slick dancer, and played the dandy with the girls.

These social activities opened the gate of opportunity. Samish and the San Francisco tax collector belonged to the same social club, and the collector, charmed by the lad, gave him a job in his office. It was Samish's first big break, his introduction into the world of politics.

In the three years he spent in the tax collector's office, young Artie Samish got an insider's view of the mechanics of political opera-tions. Eyes and ears always open, the youngster sopped up knowledge that would be invaluable to him in the future.

Job led to job as political connections on the lower rungs of the ladder provided the impetus for step-ups to higher positions. Samish moved to the state capital in Sacramento, where he found work in the Division of Motor Vehicles. Then he became a page in the assembly, running errands for the assemblymen; history clerk of the lower house; and finally, at twenty-three, the engrossing and enrolling clerk for the entire legislature. In these various roles, he met practically everyone of consequence in the state's political life, including a young lawyer from Oakland named Earl Warren, who later was to become governor of the state and, finally, Chief Justice of the United States.

It was almost inevitable that a hard runner with such contacts should become a lobbyist. Samish's first venture into this new field came around 1922 or 1923, when an attorney who represented trading-stamp interests became tired of battling independent grocers, who sought to get a law passed banning such stamp bonuses by the larger stores. Each year Frank Connolly, the lobbyist for the independent grocers, per-suaded the legislature to vote such a ban—and each year his opposition, using its influence with the governor, got the bill vetoed.

Jesse H. Steinhart, the attorney who represented trading-stamp interests in this war of lobbyist against lobbyist, asked Samish if he would like to take over the job. "Sure—what the hell!" Samish replied, and with those words he was launched on a new career.

Right from the start, Samish used the technique that was to make him the dominant political power in the state. First he set out to discover how each legislator stood on the trading-stamp issue. He drove all over the state for heart-to-heart talks with senators and assemblymen. Then he visited the chain stores and trading-stamp interests he represented.

His proposition was simple: through his researches, he had learned who was "safe" for trading stamps and who was not. The next step was obvious: the trading-stamp interests must raise a fund to ensure the reelection of their friends and the defeat of their enemies. Samish's employers, impressed by this irrefutable logic, put up the money, Samish dispensed it where it would do the most good—and never again did the legislature of California pass a bill banning trading stamps.

Samish in later life expressed only contempt for the crude operators who sought to intimidate legislators or buy their votes. His system was much more basic and had the beauty of simplicity: "Select and Elect." As he told Bob Thomas, "I simply selected those men I thought would be friendly to my clients' interests. Then I saw to it that those men got elected to the legislature."

If one of the chosen later exhibited bad judgment and didn't vote the way Samish wanted, Samish punished him for the indiscretion by using the same kind of financial clout that had helped elect him to make certain he wasn't reelected when he had to run again. Samish explained his political philosophy, if one can call it that, this way: "I didn't care whether a man was a Republican or a Democrat or a Prohibitionist. I didn't care whether he voted against free love and for the boll weevil. All I cared about was how he voted on legislation affecting my clients."

When Samish said he didn't care whether a man was a Prohibitionist, he must have had tongue in cheek, for the liquor interests had supplied the funds for the political war chest that made Samish an uncrowned king. Samish began representing the California State Brewers Association in 1935, and from the start he employed the same tactics he had used in his first lobbying skirmish on the trading-stamp issue.

He persuaded the brewers to tax themselves five cents on every barrel of heady dew they produced. The resulting kitty supplied Samish personally with a basic fee of $30,000 a year, and it put $150,000 into a so-called educational fund that Samish could use wherever it would do the most good.

Samish's representation of the brewers was so successful that soon he had the entire liquor industry united behind him. This meant additional muscle. Samish reasoned it out this way: there were fifty thousand liquor outlets in the state; each, counting employees and their relatives, represented an average of ten votes. That meant half a million votes—and this was only the beginning. Each liquor outlet had hundreds of customers. If the majority of these could be persuaded to vote "right" on a given candidate or issue, the resulting political power would be awesome. To help the campaign of persuasion along, there were more than four thousand billboards controlled by the liquor interests, and at election time these billboards could be used to display Samish's cleverly concocted political propaganda.

The manner in which Samish developed and used all these resources was vividly demonstrated in his years-long running battle with the Drys. Though Prohibition had been repealed, the foes of liquor had not surrendered, and in 1936 they got enough signatures to a petition to place on the ballot a constitutional amendment providing for local option in the state. If this was approved by the voters, it would mean that every municipal governing body would have the power, if it wished, to ban the sale of alcohol within its jurisdiction. The threat to the liquor industry was obvious.

In this crisis, Samish adopted what was to become for him a favorite strategy. Whenever a measure odious to his employers got on the ballot, he made certain that a countermeasure was placed before the voters at the same election. That way, one measure might cancel out the other or, at least, so confuse the voters that both would be defeated, leaving the status quo undisturbed.

Wily Samish realized that his own proposition stood the best chance of passage if it stood high on the sometimes long list of measures on which the electorate was asked to pass judgment. The first three positions on the ballot were the prime attention-getters. If voters had to wade through a long list of propositions after that, their interest flagged, they became confused, and they frequently gave up the attempt to reach a decision. Having cultivated the right friends in the right places, Samish was usually able to perform the miracle of getting his favored measure in one of those top three slots.

The 1936 battle over the Drys' local-option referendum illustrated the beauties of Samish's double strategy. The Drys' amendment was relegated to the ninth position on the ballot; Samish's anti-Dry measure was number three. In the campaign for public support, Samish

spent a lot of the liquor industry's money in two ways—to rally support
for number three, and to whip up opposition to number nine. As a
result, the electorate became so confused that both propositions were
defeated, an outcome that was in effect a victory for Samish and the
liquor barons because it left everything just the way it had been in the
beginning.

Nevertheless, the die-hard Prohibitionists did not give up. In
1948 they returned to the war with another local-option initiative. This
time, Samish got his countermeasure placed on the ballot as number
two; the Drys' proposition was sunk way down in the twelfth slot. This
time, too, Samish was determined to crush the anti-liquor forces so
badly they would never pose a threat again.

He raised an enormous $750,000 campaign fund from the big
manufacturers and wholesalers. Then he contacted the fifty thousand
liquor licensees in the state. He didn't want money, he told them; he
just wanted them to get out and work in their districts to drum up
opposition to the new Prohibitionist threat.

Bankrolled and backed in this manner, the Samish propaganda
machine outdid itself. Samish obtained a picture of a mother—"the
most beautiful mother you ever did see"—in a gingham dress, with a
broom in her hand. The picture was plastered on billboards and appeared in newspaper advertisements throughout the state. It was cap-
tioned: "LET'S CLEAN THEM OUT—VOTE YES ON NUMBER TWO!"

"That didn't have a damn thing to do with the proposition, but
it sure as hell attracted a lot of sympathy," Samish recalled later.

The campaign for number two was matched by an equally
strenuous campaign against the Drys' number twelve. In the end, both
measures were defeated, but the Drys' anti-liquor option was drowned
in a hostile tidal wave. More votes were cast on this proposition than on
any other on the ballot—and number twelve was trounced in all fifty-
eight counties in the state. The annihilating totals were 2,598,815 votes
against to 1,025,941 in favor, a margin of better than two to one. Never
again were the Drys able to mount a threat to the liquor industry in
California.

Samish later boasted that in the twenty years he represented the
brewers the state tax on beer never increased. Real estate taxes, gasoline
taxes, literally all taxes went up during those two decades, but the
brewery tax remained pegged at sixty-two cents on each thirty-one-gal-
lon barrel. Occasionally some idealist in the legislature would propose

that the brewers be made to share the people's increasing tax burdens, but whenever that happened, Samish—"the governor of the legislature"—saw to it that the higher tax bill never got out of committee.

How did Samish always, unfailingly, perform such magic? The secret lay, of course, in the success of his formula: "Select and Elect." He selected and elected so well that he created a unique phenomenon on the American political scene: he built what was in effect a separate political party—a lobbyist's party—that cut across Republican and Democratic lines, its members beholden to the power of the Samish campaign purse that had done so much to elect them.

Carey McWilliams, soon to become editor of *The Nation*, analyzed the Samish political empire in a July, 1949, *Nation* profile that preceded and probably inspired the Lester Velie *Collier's* series.

"What Mr. Samish has done," McWilliams wrote, "is to convert the interest-group into a political machine which functions independently of the party. From the lobbyists' point of view, of course, this represents a distinct advance in the forms of political control. A party machine can be challenged at the polls but as long as Artie controls the interest-groups, his power is beyond dispute.

"Theoretically his power could be challenged by the interest-groups he represents but—and this is the key to the structure of power he has fashioned—these groups enjoy, despite the costs, great advantages from his representation.

"In the first place, the state takes over the function and also the expense of policing the particular industry against 'unfair trade practices'—an enormous saving in itself. In the second place, each industry-group and each individual member is spared the trouble and expense of dealing with individual politicians."

It was not necessary for Samish to elect a majority of the legislature for him to wield such power. In state legislatures as in the national Congress, the key to legislation lies in the work performed out of the public view in committees. A bill, when it is introduced, is referred to the particular committee appointed to study such legislation. There it can die a quiet death, or, if the committee favors it, it is reported out to the floor for action. Thus control of key committees becomes vitally important to the lobbyist. Carey McWilliams discussed the manner in which Samish acquired and exercised such control.

"From 1931 to the present time," he wrote, "Samish has controlled a large bloc of votes in the state legislature. Control of this bloc is tantamount to control of the legislature, as this bloc usually elects the Speaker, who appoints the committees."

The man who wielded such power had acquired a ballooning paunch from years of high living. He was a broad-featured, wiseacrish individual, jovial and gregarious, the lover and giver of uproarious parties. At the height of his power in the 1940s, he and his wife, the former Merced Sullivan, had two beautiful homes, one in San Francisco and a larger spread down the California peninsula. Ever the genial host, Artie Samish thought nothing of throwing a bash for some two hundred to three hundred guests at a time. "I'd really put on a show for those folks," he told Bob Thomas later.

His headquarters when the legislature was in session was a lavish suite, number 428, in the Senator Hotel, directly across the street from the capitol in Sacramento. The refrigerator was always full of steaks and beer, and the welcome sign was always out for hungry and thirsty legislators. From this combination office and hospitality suite, Samish directed a staff of about twenty-five operatives (the "Gestapo" about whom he had boasted to Velie) whose duty it was to keep an hourly check on legislative actions that might affect the welfare of any of Samish's numerous clients.

The boss lobbyist himself put in a superhuman working day. He rose at about 11 A.M., conferred with his "Gestapo," gave each member his assignments. Then the tempo of the day stepped up, becoming more hectic by the minute as telephone calls chased one another over the buzzing wires. Samish was constantly on the phone, taking reports from his men in the capitol, giving instructions, calling contacts and clients throughout the state—and, indeed, throughout much of the nation.

From eleven to eleven, he hardly stopped talking into the telephone mouthpiece as he asked questions, assessed various situations, and fired off instructions for dealing with them. Then, with midnight approaching, he would leave the scene of the day's confusion and go downstairs to the lobby of the hotel, where he would hobnob with politicians, judges, commissioners, cops, secretaries, reporters, clerks, bookies—and, of course, a whole swarm of fellow lobbyists representing every interest from teachers to railroads, oil, power companies, and retailers. Samish's advice was freely given to those who sought it as he held a kind of royal court in the hotel lobby until four o'clock in the morning, when he would finally fall into bed.

At the end of every legislative session, the thirty-five best-heeled lobbyists in Sacramento contributed one hundred dollars each to defray the expenses of a legislative ball, a real shindig for the forty senators and eighty assemblymen and their wives. Artie Samish was always the master of ceremonies. One of his agents who lobbied on behalf of the movie studios would bring in a bunch of stars from Hollywood for entertainment, and the Governor's Hall at the state fairgrounds would rock with the festivities until the early morning hours.

Samish, as the moving spirit of the affair, naturally had charge of the seating arrangements, and he took unabashed pleasure in the opportunity this gave him both to reward and to express his displeasure. "Those who were friends got ringside seats in front of the entertainment," he later explained. "Those who had failed to display their friendship found themselves seated behind a potted palm."

Even when the legislature disbanded and its members scattered to their homes, Samish's frenetic life-style continued at an unabated pace. Once he summoned an entire band and flew the astonished members off to Alaska, where the governor was holding a big party and needed some music. His usual itinerary crisscrossed the nation: Florida in season; Hot Springs, Arkansas, for the baths; Louisville for the Kentucky Derby; New York to meet liquor mogul Lewis Rosenstiel and to give helpful advice to William O'Dwyer, then running for mayor.

Artie Samish's influence was virtually limitless during the two decades, 1930–50, when he dominated the California legislature. Sacramento swarmed with lobbyists during those years. The *San Francisco Chronicle* reported in 1949 that 364 were registered (which gave them the right to appear before legislative committees), and that there were probably as many more who were not registered. This swarm of influence-peddlers, each representing a special interest, swirled around Artie Samish, the one man above all others who knew how to get things done.

Many industries, of course, hired the champion doer directly. Typical were the bus and trucking interests, among Samish's earliest clients. As early as 1924 two executives of a San Francisco bus line sought Samish's help. The railroads, especially the powerful Southern Pacific, were attempting to tax the motor carriers out of existence. Though the railroad lobby in Sacramento had been discredited by its past excesses, the rail barons still exercised vast influence across the state and were able to get individual towns and cities through which bus lines passed to impose high taxes on the carriers. Tax was thus piled upon tax until the bus operators feared they would be taxed into bankruptcy. Their only solution, as they saw it, was to get the state to set a uniform fee, relieving them of multiple gouging by local governing bodies.

Samish realized at once that a single bus line could not fight the railroad interests, and that what was needed was a unified carrier organization, representing both bus and trucking lines and so wielding muscle for the entire over-the-road industry. As he always did in such situations, Samish went on tour, educating the owners of other bus lines about the reality that confronted them and the virtues of united effort. The result was the formation of the Motor Carriers Association, with Samish as secretary-treasurer. In effect, he *was* the association.

Having united competing lines in a common effort, Samish got the legislature to pass an act making all bus operations full-fledged public utilities under the jurisdiction of the Railroad Commission, soon to be known as the Public Utilities Commission. Next he got a proposition placed on the ballot giving the state sole right to tax bus and truck lines.

The railroads, naturally, threw all their monetary and political resources into the battle to defeat the measure. Samish argued that seventeen hundred communities in the state depended solely on bus transportation and that the railroads (no public benefactors) were simply trying to crush competition. The argument on the merits of the case failed to register with the voters, who trounced the state tax proposal by a 70,000-vote margin.

Undeterred, Samish returned to the field at the next election. This time, he decided, he wouldn't just reason with the voters; he would propagandize them. He hired Johnny Argens, a well-known cartoonist, to draw "a picture of a big, fat, ugly pig." This gross caricature was then plastered on billboards throughout the state with the slogan DRIVE THE HOG FROM THE ROAD! VOTE YES ON PROPOSITION NUMBER 2.

Millions of handbills were printed bearing the same picture and message. They were placed in automobiles in every city and town. The repulsive hog aroused the ire of voters as no amount of argument would have done—and Samish's constitutional amendment passed by an overwhelming 700,000-vote margin. Bus lines and truckers were freed from multiple local taxation, the buses paying the state a 4.5 percent tax, the trucks 5 percent. Both types of carriers also got free license plates. "All because," as Samish later chortled, "the voters thought they were voting against roadhogs."

The motor carriers were so pleased that Samish ran the affairs of their association for thirty years—at a handsome retainer, of course. There was another bonus: Samish, having gained some inside knowledge about the busing industry, saw and seized an opportunity that made him independently wealthy.

The huge Greyhound line had begun to buy out and absorb many of the smaller, competing independent systems. Samish realized that if he could get control of some of these branch routes, he might be able to dispose of them to acquisitive Greyhound at a handsome profit. There was one difficulty: he had no money with which to finance such a venture.

As always, however, he had contacts. He and A. P. Giannini, founder and president of the gigantic Bank of America, knew each other well and would sometimes meet on their way to their offices and stand talking on a street corner. Taking advantage of this friendship, Samish went to see Giannini and explained his idea. "I'll give you the money," Giannini said. The result: in nine months, without investing a cent of his own, Samish acquired several meshing bus lines, boosted their operating profits—and then sold them to Greyhound for more than a million dollars. His own net profit was a handsome $290,000.

Even in the act of raking in the money from his coup, Artie Samish proved one thing: he personally was no roadhog. Art Smith, head of the Yellow Cab Company, had given Samish invaluable advice and had helped him set up the deal. Before the transaction with Greyhound was consummated, however, Smith died. His savings had been practically wiped out in the 1929 Wall Street stock market crash, and he left his widow, Rosabel, nearly destitute. Samish had no legal obligation to pay Smith's estate anything, but he decided to split his windfall with the widow, sending her $145,000, half of his profits. It was an act that Smith's successor as president of Yellow Cab later called "one of the most extraordinary instances of magnanimity, unselfishness, integrity of character, idealism and loyalty to friendship ever to come to my attention."

The bankers of California also profited indirectly from A. P. Giannini's generosity to the man who could get things done. During the Great Depression of the 1930s, the banks had had to foreclose mortgages on properties that could be disposed of only at distressed prices. Yet, according to California law, they had no more than five years in which to rid themselves of such holdings.

Parker Maddux, then president of the San Francisco Bank, became concerned as the depression dragged on and on. If his bank had to sell foreclosed properties in such bad times, it would lose literally millions of dollars. He went to Samish. Under the existing law, he said, his bank would have to dispose of "between thirty and forty million dollars worth of real estate" at "a substantial loss."

Samish agreed to help the banks. The solution, it appeared to him, was almost ridiculously simple. He had the State Banking Law—"a volume big enough to kill a rat with"—printed up with just one amending change. It involved a single word, the substitution of "ten" for "five" in the number of years' grace granted the banks in disposing of foreclosed properties. This little, almost imperceptible change attracted no hostile notice, and the revised act sailed through both houses of the legislature by unanimous votes. Yet that alteration of one word had saved the San Francisco Bank alone about twenty million dollars.

★

It was inevitable, human nature being what it is, that a man who exercised the kind of influence and power Artie Samish did should run afoul of others whose power drives conflicted with his own. One who caused Samish trouble was Governor Frank Merriam, a confirmed Prohibitionist. When Samish got the legislature to pass a bill raising the salaries of members of the Liquor Control Board, he and Merriam collided. Merriam said he would veto the bill, and Samish quotes himself as telling the governor, "Why you bald-headed son of a bitch, I helped get you into that governor's chair. And I'll get your ass out of it, too."

Merriam, Samish says in one of the understatements of the age, "didn't take too kindly" to this blunt defiance and retaliated by mounting a crusade to investigate lobbyists—and one lobbyist in particular. On the last day of the 1937 session, the legislature authorized the probe and appropriated $50,000 to finance it. "I let Merriam have it—I had nothing to hide," Samish records.

District Attorney Otis D. Babcock, of Sacramento County, conducted the probe and hired Howard R. Philbrick as an investigator. Artie Samish, the old hell-raiser, took it all as an enticing game—it added spice to his life. And he got an impish pleasure out of baiting Philbrick and Babcock the way a matador baits a bull.

"I knew he [Philbrick] was bugging my office and telephone," Samish later told Bob Thomas. "So every time I walked into my office, I said quite loudly, 'Good morning, Mr. Philbrick.' And when I answered the phone, I said, 'Now listen to this, Mr. Philbrick.' "

Since the real purpose of the Merriam campaign against lobbyists was to "get" Samish, Artie was subpoenaed to appear before the grand jury. He was willing enough, and he even sought and got an unprecedented agreement that his questioning would be conducted in public, not in the customary inviolate secrecy of the grand jury room. The public hearing gave Samish the opportunity to strut in the headlines and do all possible damage to Merriam, who was running for reelection at the time.

To expose the governor and his motives, Samish produced two photographs. He exhibited them to reporters before he turned them over to the district attorney. Merriam, unfortunately for him, had inscribed the pictures "to a pal, Art Samish." Samish also produced letters in which the governor had thanked him for his great assistance during the 1934 gubernatorial campaign. It was all quite embarrassing for Merriam, who was attempting to don white crusader's robes in his joust against the man he pictured as the evil genius in the state.

Samish had sport with District Attorney Babcock, too. He was also seeking reelection, and Samish, hearing of a promising law school graduate who might make a good opposition candidate, backed the virtual unknown, plastering all Sacramento with signs that read: HONEST MCDOUGAL FOR DISTRICT ATTORNEY.

Babcock squeaked to a narrow victory, but the "honest McDougal" campaign, with its inevitable implication that perhaps he wasn't McDougal's equal in virtue, so infuriated Babcock that he challenged Samish in the witness stand.

"You know a whole lot about the McDougal campaign, don't you?" he demanded.

"If I had only had two or three days longer, I would have known more," Samish told him.

"But you didn't do it," Babcock sneered.

"No, but two or three more days and you wouldn't have been standing there as district attorney," Samish retorted.

In the end, the much-trumpeted lobbying probe caged no lions. Philbrick, in his final report, said some harsh things about Artie Samish, but Samish was immune to the pinpricks of verbal criticism. Philbrick reported that "all investigative roads" led to Samish; that Samish represented "motor carrier, liquor, racing, theatrical and other interests"; that investigators had traced a cash flow of $496,138.62 through Samish bank accounts in just the three years between 1935 and 1938—and that they were convinced they hadn't uncovered all of Samish's financial resources. It was all just words, words, words—and Samish could afford to laugh at them.

Frank Merriam had no such cause for merriment. Samish threw all the resources of his liquor industry network into the campaign to defeat the governor, and he made good his boast that he would boot Merriam out of his governor's chair. Even this success didn't quite appease Samish.

Merriam tried to maintain his position as the most prominent California Republican, the titular head of the party. In the 1940 contest for the Republican presidential nomination, Merriam favored Ohio's veteran U.S. senator, Robert A. Taft, but a lot of younger party members were fascinated by the dark-horse candidacy of Wendell Willkie. The split within the party gave Artie Samish the chance to deliver the coup de grace to his old foe Merriam.

"I didn't give a hoot about presidential politics," he said years later. "But I enjoyed doing anything to knock down Frank Merriam."

He decided, in effect, to take the state Republican convention away from Merriam. The focal point was the selection of a state central committeeman to greet Willkie when he came to California on a speech-making tour. Samish had spotted a capable young assemblyman, Thomas H. Kuchel, and he decided that Kuchel should make the race against Merriam.

Leaving nothing to chance, Samish recruited one hundred high school students at two dollars each to pack the galleries and jeer every mention of Merriam's name, cheer every mention of Kuchel's. When Merriam appeared in the convention hall, he was greeted by such a resounding volume of hooting and catcalls that "his bald head turned lobster red." When the vote was taken, Samish cashed in a lot of IOU's he had acquired among the delegates, and man after man on whom Merriam had counted switched sides and voted for Kuchel. The defeat crushed Merriam, who, in Samish's words, "slunk back to Long Beach and was never heard from again." Conversely, the contest was the making of Thomas Kuchel, who went on to become one of the more distinguished members of the U.S. Senate.

The man who could make and unmake a governor was, indeed, as was often said, "the guy who gets things done" in California. He could get so much done with the waving of his financial wand that, in one of the more incredible episodes in his career, he picked up a drifter, a bum, and catapulted him into a seat in the California Assembly.

Early in 1934 Samish got a telephone call from his man in Los Angeles, Bill Jasper. Jasper told him that one of their most important clients, a wealthy brewer, wanted to put a candidate into the field against Clair Woolwine, scion of one of the oldest and most distinguished families of Los Angeles and a longtime assemblyman from the city's downtown district. It sounded insane to Samish, since Woolwine appeared unbeatable, but Jasper said the big brewer was nursing a personal grudge against Woolwine and was determined to give him at least a scare. To accomplish this, he was willing to finance an opposition campaign.

"We have to satisfy his whims," Samish told Jasper. "Get him a candidate."

Where? How? Samish didn't know; just do it, he said.

Desperate, Jasper went to the headquarters of novelist Upton Sinclair, who was then trying to get the Democratic nomination for governor on what the established order considered his radical End Poverty in California platform. The headquarters was in a dingy old store, where about forty derelicts were bundling up campaign literature for mailing.

Jasper asked if any of them were from Woolwine's forty-fourth Assembly District.

"I am," said one of the least prepossessing of the lot.

He was a tatterdemalion figure, starvation thin, with a mouthful of bad teeth and a strange accent. Jasper asked if he were an American citizen, and the man, John Pelletier, said indignantly that he was. He had been born in Maine, had graduated from Bates College, but had grown up in Montreal, where he had acquired a French-Canadian accent.

"How'd you like to run for the state legislature?" Jasper asked.

Pelletier stared as if he thought Jasper had just escaped from a mental hospital, but the lobbyist assured him he was serious. In a daze, Pelletier followed Jasper to a restaurant. There Jasper bought a hot meal, which Pelletier wolfed down with the eagerness of a man wanting to make certain of this bounty before his crazy escort came to his senses.

From the restaurant Jasper dragged his unlikely protégé to a tailor shop where he bought Pelletier two suits, underwear, shoes, ties —all the accessories to make him at least presentable. The next stop was the Luxor Baths, where Jasper instructed an attendant to shave, bathe, and clean up the scarecrow about to become politician. When this transformation to cleanliness had been achieved, Pelletier looked, if not imposing, at least halfway respectable.

When Jasper telephoned Samish and described these events, the boss lobbyist almost fell out of his chair, his huge sides shaking with laughter. The zaniness of the thing was something that fun-loving, prankster-prone Artie Samish could really relish. Go ahead, he told Jasper. Pelletier might at least give Woolwine a few anxious moments, and this was all their big-brewer client really expected of them. "We'll have a lot of laughs with this one," Artie predicted.

As it turned out, they had a lot more than laughs. Pelletier had a picture of himself that had been taken twenty-five years before, when he was in college, and Jasper superimposed the youthful-looking photograph against a background shot of the state capitol. He had a hundred thousand handbills printed and distributed. Posters featuring Pelletier's name and the deceptive photograph went up all over the district—and, miracle of miracles, the scarecrow whom Jasper had snatched off the relief rolls won the Democratic nomination!

That was certainly worth a laugh as a starter, but by this time Jasper had become hooked on his own hoax. He still had the larger part of the brewer's $2,000 campaign contribution left and, with Samish's approval, he put it into the fall campaign against Woolwine. Times were still hard in 1934, with the country not able to shake off the effects of the worst depression in history, and Pelletier walked around his district, canvassing for votes among persons like himself who knew what it was like to be out of work and hopeless. He was much closer to the times and the electorate than the well-born, aristocratic Clair Woolwine, and when the votes were counted, Jasper and Samish were stunned to discover that they had transformed their pickup derelict into a state assemblyman.

Amazingly, Pelletier in office turned out to be a credit to the lobbyists who had made him. He was no fool—he had done a lot of reading in his solitary life, and he voted his conscience. He was reelected time and again until he served five terms in the assembly before he died in 1945. "Always he was for the poor, the downtrodden—quite naturally because he was one of them," Samish later recalled. "And why shouldn't the poor have their own representative in the assembly? I thought it was a dandy idea."

Pelletier had just one phobia: he detested lawyers. Since most members of the legislature belonged to the legal profession, he had a lot to detest, and sometimes, when he became annoyed beyond endurance at the legalistic wrangling over fine points, he would leap up and shout without waiting to be recognized by the presiding officer:

"Mr. Speaker, there are too many goddamned lawyers in this assembly! I am going to introduce a constitutional amendment which will limit the number of lawyers who can serve in this body."

Though there were many among the poor and downtrodden who probably felt very much as Pelletier did, their lone representative in an assembly swarming with members of the denounced profession could never rally any support for such an unorthodox proposal.

★

Such was the pervasive power of Artie Samish, such the prodigies he performed for his clients during the more than twenty years that he was the real power behind the public facade of California politics. Then, at the zenith, Artie Samish went and blew the whistle on himself in those outrageously frank interviews with Lester Velie.

Why did he do it? A man as astute as Samish certainly knew there would be a terrible ruckus when it got out that he had bragged he was "the governor of the legislature" and had even offered to unscrew the cupola atop the capitol dome. Why, then?

Samish's explanation is that his mother, whom he had worshiped from boyhood, had died in 1948. Depressed, he was perhaps the victim of a politically suicidal death wish. "Maybe I was looking for a way out," he theorized years later. "Maybe the fun had gone out of being 'the secret boss of California.' Maybe I just didn't have the heart for it any more."

Whatever his reasons, the *Collier's* articles were an acute public embarrassment for every politician in California from the minnow to the whale. Red-faced members of the legislature were naturally indignant and had to defend their honor after being pictured as Artie's stooges. No less embarrassed was the state's foremost politician, Governor Earl Warren, who had admitted to Velie: "On matters that affect his clients, Artie unquestionably has more power than the governor."

Legislators orated and beat their breasts and raged at the imputation they were a lobbyist's pawns. They practically fell over one another introducing high-principled bills to put an end to the heinous influence of lobbyists. The trouble was, however, that such measures couldn't really be effective unless the lawyer-legislators against whom John Pelletier had raged were willing to make some sacrifices themselves. For example, one widely practiced method of influencing a lawyer-legislator was to hire him at a handsome retainer to appear as counsel for a business firm or industry group needing the goodwill of some state agency. As a consequence, legislators shuddered with horror at a reform bill that provided "no elective or appointive officer of the state can represent a client before any agency of the administration or the legislature."

It was unthinkable that reform should go *that* far, and so bill after bill was watered down. The sound and fury of the righteous but unwilling filled the newspapers; nothing effective was accomplished —and Artie Samish continued doing business at the same old stand.

He had, however, made enemies with elephantine memories. Earl Warren, three times elected governor, was running hard for President, and it did his image no good for the self-proclaimed "governor of the legislature" to remain untouched and untouchable. Warren lost the 1952 Republican presidential nomination to Dwight D. Eisenhower, a national hero, who made him chief justice of the United States. An influential figure in the party, Warren placed some of his protégés in important posts in the new administration, and one of them, Warren Olney III, became head of the criminal division in the U.S. attorney general's office.

The Justice Department had investigated Samish after the Kefauver exposé of 1950 and had found no legal ground for prosecution. But Olney, who had clashed with Samish before, prodded Internal Revenue to reopen the case. Confident he had always operated within the letter of the law, Samish opened all his books and records to the Internal Revenue sleuths. They spent some two years ferreting, and, finally, to Samish's great surprise, they found something they could hang on him.

Samish's version is this: in the 1940s he had recommended a public relations agent whom he knew to Lewis Rosenstiel, president of Schenley Industries, one of the great liquor combines. With the help of this push from Artie, the public relations man had acquired the remunerative Schenley account. Grateful, he passed the word through underlings that he wanted to reward his helper. Samish insisted he didn't want any money for dropping the right word in the right ear, but the public relations man was insistent. Oh, well, Samish said in effect, if he wants to give his money away, let him help some political friends of mine. Checks were made out to various persons whom Samish named, but—and here was the legal catch—they were turned over to Artie to distribute. Years later, in 1953, Internal Revenue contended that since Samish had had physical possession of the checks, even though they weren't made out to him, they were income for which he should have accounted. He was accused of evading taxes on $71,878.

Samish couldn't believe it, but a trial jury did. He was convicted, and the conviction was upheld by the U.S. Court of Appeals. Higher up, the Supreme Court of Earl Warren refused to consider the case, and Samish was sentenced to three years in federal prison and fined $40,000. In addition, Internal Revenue charged that he had to pay taxes on the money he had handled for the Brewers' Fund, and he finally settled this claim by paying Uncle Sam $919,374.

Samish spent twenty-six months in McNeil Island penitentiary in the state of Washington. Released in March, 1958, he returned to San Francisco. He was finished with politics, finished with lobbying— but far from finished personally. His income tax troubles, legal fees, and penalties had cost him well over one million dollars, but he was not impoverished. He had, he reported, "some investments left. A few oil wells here and there. I built a couple of hotels in Palm Springs. And I had been retired with a comfortable pension by the Brewers Institute." He also engaged in some import-export enterprises and devoted more attention to his wife, two daughters, and seven grandchildren. Life, he found, could still be fun.

When he thought about the future of lobbying, he concluded that it would go on and on unless the people take more interest in the people they elect. If citizens don't even know the names of their senators and assemblymen, much less their records and what they stand for, the way of the lobbyist remains little changed—a subtle and secretive route to privilege and favoritism and high rewards.

In the early days of the nation, there were no such words as "lobbying" or "lobbyist." There was, of course, much behind-the-scenes influence-peddling, much insidious maneuvering to gain private objectives. The practice existed at the time of the First Continental Congress before the outbreak of the Revolution, but it was a sporadic operation, depending largely on social contacts and personal friendships, real or cultivated. It did not have about it those aspects of outright pressure and subtle, corrupt rewards that have characterized much lobbying during the last one hundred and fifty years of American history.

The contrast between then and now is perhaps best illustrated by the manner in which John and Samuel Adams were wined and dined when they traveled from Boston to Philadelphia in 1774. Boston had lighted the torch of resistance to the British crown when a band of patriots, poorly disguised as Indians, had dumped a shipload of tea into the harbor in dramatic protest against taxes imposed from abroad. When the British government responded by closing the port and quartering an army on the city, Boston and all Massachusetts moved toward rebellion. Thus the two Adamses, as leaders of the patriot faction, were recognized as important and influential men who could help to dampen the fires of radicalism or to move the nation toward an outright break with the mother country.

Patriots and conservatives vied with each other to do them honor, to fete them and try to sway them toward the political

2

THE BEGINNINGS

faith of their hosts of the moment. They were honored with such a round of elaborate breakfasts, dinners, and receptions in New York that John Adams complained he had little time to visit King's College (now Columbia University) and exchange views with some of the day's intellectuals, in whom he was more interested than he was in most of the guests he met at social affairs.

New York's version of society persuasion was soon eclipsed by the reception the Massachusetts delegates were given when they arrived in Philadelphia. They were met on the outskirts of the budding capital by a cavalcade of horsemen sent especially to do them honor. From that moment on, they were caught up in an almost ceaseless round of discussions in the city's taverns and the homes of the wealthy. Many of these sessions lasted into the early morning hours, and John Adams, often a testy man, became so surfeited with wine and windy talk that he complained of his exhaustion and disgust in letters to his beloved wife, Abigail.

Karl Schriftgiesser, in his scholarly study of lobbying, described the Philadelphia scene in these words:

"All through the sessions of the Congress lobbying went on in full force. The hogsheads of Madeira and port wine that were dispensed and the huge dinners of mutton and pork, duck and turkey, fools [fruit stewed or crushed and mixed with milk, cream, or custard] and tarts and jellies, that were served by Negro manservants on tables white with linen and bright with English silver, were not offered without a purpose. The merchants, the landowners, the Quakers, the followers of the powerful John Dickinson, used all the wiles of wealth and social prestige to prevent the delegates from the other colonies from insisting upon any drastic action that might endanger the colonial way of life."

With the drafting of the Constitution in 1787, a strong central government was created with the power to dispense or withhold valuable favors. It was inevitable that, as selfish forces began to appreciate the opportunities, pressures would mount to influence government and get it to exercise its varied and immense powers for private enrichment.

The new government had hardly been established before the process began. The first tariff act was passed in 1789, and this was the occasion for a kind of lobbying effort that has continued to the present day. Each budding American industry wanted high import duties imposed on foreign goods as a means of limiting competition in its particular field. The rationalization, far more justified then than in later years, was that infant American manufacturing trades needed such protection against cheap imports if we were ever to build our own industrial society. George Washington's first secretary of the treasury, Alexander Hamilton, brilliant leader of the conservative-business bloc, formed the Society for the Protection of National Industry in the early 1800s. It might well be called the first organized business lobby, aimed at influencing state and national legislatures; and it was, in essence, the ancestor of one of the most powerful lobbies on the modern American scene—the National Association of Manufacturers, founded in 1895.

Despite this early record of special-interest pressure, government in the early days of the republic remained relatively more free and open, less dominated by selfish intrigues, than it later became. Not everyone had joined the party. The words "lobbying" and "lobbyists" had not yet become part of our language, and private agents seeking special favors for their clients at the expense of all others had not yet descended like swarms of locusts on state and national capitals.

H. L. Mencken, the Baltimore sage who traced the origins of common American terms, found that the word "lobby" came into use here for the first time in 1829, the year Andrew Jackson became President. The first references Mencken found were to "lobby-agents," and they referred to influence-wielders around the New York State capitol in Albany. Journalists soon shortened the awkward "lobby-agent" to plain "lobbyist," and by 1832 the new term was in widespread use in Washington. From the beginning, it was generally considered a term of opprobrium. Walt Whitman, the poet, cried out against ". . . brawling office-holders . . . kept editors, bribers, compromisers, lobbiers, spongers . . . the lousy combines and born freedom-sellers of the earth."

The history of the times amply justified such vitriol. True, the nation was being transformed from pigmy into giant during that last half of the nineteenth century. Railroads linked the nation from coast to coast. Great industries were being built, and these in time would make America a world power. Most Americans took a patriotic pride in these achievements, in this flexing of the national muscle, and they remained blind to the cost. But the cost was great.

The corruption of public life on many levels was all but complete. Professor Robert Rienow and his wife, Leona, have described in their book *Of Snuff, Sin and the Senate* the nearly total corruption of the U.S. Senate in the 1890s and early 1900s. E. H. Harriman, one of the early railroad magnates, openly boasted: "If I choose, I can buy the

Congress and the entire judiciary." And the Senate itself, the main citadel of special privilege, was so rotten it was described in the press here and abroad as "the Senate of Shame."

It was a Senate that granted more privileges to the powerful and wealthy—and blocked reforms that might have benefited the great mass of Americans about whom President Truman later worried. Scottish critic William Archer described the United States of this period as "an enormously rich country overrun by a horde of robber barons." And he pointed out that there was "no income tax, no inheritance tax, no compensation for workmen killed on the job, no restrictions of importance for the protection of women and children, and even local laws seeking workmen's compensation were killed ungraciously by the Federal courts."

Such was the influence of the heavily financed lobbies during these formative decades that determined the pattern of American life. By contrast, lobbyists for social causes struggled along on barren budgets and time and again found their best efforts frustrated by the power of their well-heeled adversaries.

Typical of the idealistic and self-sacrificing breed that tried to promote the people's causes was Benjamin C. Marsh. The son of missionary parents, he lobbied for a wide variety of common-good issues for forty-three years, beginning in 1907. In his book, Lobbyist for the People, Marsh described how he struggled along on budgets that never averaged more than a pitiful $8,500 a year.

Many of the interests he attacked considered him a radical, yet a list of the causes for which he lobbied indicates that in many instances he was simply too far ahead of his time. He pioneered the drive for city planning and advocated such policies as progressive personal income and profits taxes; public ownership of power and other natural resources; federal old-age pensions and unemployment insurance; public works and public housing; farm resettlement projects; federal relief during the Great Depression; pure food and drug laws; civil rights; price fixing and rationing during World War II; protective labor legislation and a shorter work week (Marsh was advocating a thirty-hour week long before the election of Franklin D. Roosevelt in 1932); and international organization and cooperation.

Some of these causes triumphed, aided by the exposés of the great muckraking journalists of the early 1900s and, in some instances, by the sheer pressure of events (as in the Roosevelt administration reforms of the depression period). Others remain visionary to this day.

Marsh testified repeatedly before congressional committees, made speeches all over the country, trying to whip up public sentiment for his causes, and was the mainspring of the People's Lobby until it was disbanded in 1950. By such ceaseless activity, he sometimes made an impact, but often, in his collision with powerful entrenched forces, he resembled Don Quixote tilting with windmills.

He labored in New York City for ten years in a futile effort to curb the real estate interests by imposing a land tax that would take the profit out of speculation and, in the process, make tenements less profitable, thus reducing overcrowding and improving the health of the people. Scratching for funds as always, he secured an appointment with J. P. Morgan, the banking mogul. After Marsh explained his program, Morgan rose from his chair and said, "Young man, I've always been more interested in improving my own condition than that of other people."

"Mr. Morgan," Marsh shot back as he left the office, "I've always understood that to be the case."

Marsh opposed American involvement in World War I, a step he believed was being pressed to ensure the collection of loans Morgan and other bankers had made to Great Britain. When it became apparent that America was not going to stay out, Marsh decided that, if young Americans were going to be conscripted to fight and die, the wealth of the nation should also be conscripted to take the profit out of war and to pay for it as it was being fought. When he started to read a resolution to this effect at a Madison Square Garden rally, the result was dramatic and unexpected.

"Within two minutes," he later wrote, "three or four of the 2,000 men in uniform, whom Police Commissioner Arthur Woods had organized, were on my back or at my side; and I was hustled out to an ante-room and frisked. These toy soldiers did not find anything on me, but one of them socked me on the chin and then in the back of my neck. A plainclothes detective advised me to beat it before I was killed, and escorted me to a street car; so, as he said, 'You will have a chance to get home alive.'"

During the 1920s, Marsh lobbied in Washington against bills that turned much of the nation's remaining natural resources over to private industry, and in favor of a measure to tax excessive corporate and personal incomes more heavily. In championing the tax measure, he appeared before the Senate Finance Committee headed by Boise Penrose, of Pennsylvania. Of this encounter, he later wrote:

"I gave some startling, for those days, figures on the profits of corporation and big personal incomes, on both of which the tax was very low; and urged a sizeable increase. When I went to correct my testimony, the universal practice, I found many of my figures stricken out, which meant they wouldn't appear in the printed record of the hearing. The Clerk of the Committee explained the Chairman had ordered this and he had to comply—as of course he had to, or lose his job. Over the boy's protests, I stormed into Senator Penrose's private office and asked him by what authority he had tampered with my testimony.

" 'By my own,' he replied, quite candidly.

" 'But this isn't legal, is it?' I put up to him.

"The Harvard graduate—known as a reformer, chiefly of Philadelphia's municipal corruption, in his early post-college days—looked at me quizzically and with a perfectly refined Harvard accent, not sullied by long use in Philadelphia's vicious ward politics, replied: 'Of course it isn't legal, but you can't do a damned thing about it.' "

Such brazen and illegal elimination of testimony to protect powerful interests was a testament to the uphill battle men like Ben Marsh had to wage in attempting to lobby for the people. If, in Marsh's time, it was a decidedly uneven contest, it had been in the preceding decades virtually no contest at all. The post–Civil War period down to the turn of the century had been a halcyon period for self-interest lobbyists, and the insidious evils of the trade were never more clearly demonstrated than in the railroad-building frenzy.

The great railroad barons did indeed link the nation with iron rails from coast to coast, an achievement in which the average American of the time took uncritical pride. But the deed was accomplished through the wholesale corruption of state and national legislatures, which turned over to the promoters land empires exceeding the dimensions of many foreign countries. These free grants of public lands worth hundreds of millions of dollars underwrote railroad construction and absolved the promoters in most instances of the dire necessity of risking any of their own money. It was the greatest rip-off in American history, performed by those "bribers, compromisers, lobbiers, spongers ... and born freedom-sellers" against whom Walt Whitman had inveighed.

The most sensational lobbying effort in American history ripped off literally millions of acres of public land and turned them over as a gift to bands of stock market bandits who promised to thread the nation with connecting rail lines. The national domain in the Great West in 1850 totaled some three billion acres: rich farmlands, invaluable tracts of timber, mines of gold and silver, copper and zinc—a treasure house of untapped natural resources. Vast tracts of incalculable value, the richest of the rich, were dumped into the laps of promoters whose lobbyists sold the nation on the idea that the public good was equated with the private good of railroad manipulators.

One simple indication of the colossal giveaway may be seen in this: just four of the western railroads between 1850 and 1870 were given lands as vast as the entire territories of the large states of Ohio, Illinois, Indiana, Wisconsin, and Michigan. And this was only a part of the rip-off. Other rail lines secured equally lucrative grants. Individual states, as well as the national government, showered largesse on the heads of the promoters, voting in addition to the land grants cash subsidies running into hundreds of millions of dollars.

As a result, the stock market insiders of this licentious era reaped fortunes on every hand, finally and incidentally built railroads, and, in many instances, laughed all the way to the bank because they hadn't invested a dime of their own money. Richard P. O'Connor, in

3

THE RAILROAD RIP-OFF

his *Iron Wheels and Broken Men,* has given this vivid capsule description of the basic operation:

"First you selected a grandiose title for your operations, the Oshkosh & Pacific, for instance, even though you had barely enough capital to buy stationery and print a bond issue. Then from various state legislatures you received a charter for construction of your lines; a map showing projected construction was usually enough in those optimistic days. In return for passing out part of the bond issue to legislators and other influential citizens, you obtained land grants of alternating sections (640 acres) along your proposed right-of-way. You were rich before the first yard of ballast was tamped down. A separate land company would be established, with insiders participating. You began construction only after selling off part of the land grant and after obtaining cash subsidies from the grateful state legislature and peddling mortgage bonds in Europe. . . . The construction, too, would be undertaken by a separate company, also composed of insiders, and the rails of the Oshkosh & Pacific would be laid at an enormously inflated cost to holders of the railroad's securities. Many railroads were built without their promoters putting in a single dollar of their own money."

It would take a volume as large as a fat dictionary to catalog the activities of the horde of railway lobbyists who vied in slicing up the national domain. The way the system worked and its corruption of public officials are perhaps best exemplified in the careers of two of the leading promoters: Russell Sage, who went on to become a multimillionaire potentate of Wall Street, and George Francis Train, who perfected the bribery scheme that covered the administration of Ulysses S. Grant with scandal. Both were highly individual men—what are sometimes called "characters."

★

Sage was born August 4, 1816, in a covered wagon in which his parents, Elisha and Prudence, had been heading west. His arrival halted their journey, and the Sages settled on a heavily mortgaged farm in Durhamville in upstate New York. Life on the farm was a hard-scrabble existence, all work and no play. In later life, Russell Sage snorted, "Boyhood? I never had a boyhood. Whether we Sages fell from heaven or rose from the sea, when we got here we went to work."

These harsh childhood experiences turned boy and man into a miser. He pinched every penny and would go to almost any extreme to put behind him those early, haunting horrors of penury. He once said, "I made my millions from maxims, chief of which was the one my father favored, which went, 'Any man can earn a dollar, but it takes a wise man to keep it.' "

The boy began the keeping process early. He left home when he was only twelve and went to work in a grocery store owned by his older brother, Henry R. Sage, in Troy, New York. His salary: the princely stipend of *four dollars a month*. Out of this the boy set aside a dollar and a half for night-school classes to further his education, and every penny of the remainder was tucked away in a small chamois sack in his bedroom.

His teachers had early noted that he had "a good head for figures," and he quickly put this talent to practical use. Rivermen whose vessels docked at the wharf near his brother's store often hankered for cash to finance a spree on the town, and young Russell, delving into the cache in his chamois bag, would drive hard bargains for opera glasses, telescopes, even compasses—objects that he could resell at a handsome profit. Soon he had coins clinking in several chamois sacks, and by the time he was thirteen he had enough money to make his first real estate purchase—two lots on River Street opposite his brother's store, for which he paid $200, all in cash.

Deal led to deal as the boy, ever avid for money, constantly hunted for new ways to increase his cash reserve. He became a moneylender at exorbitant rates of interest to young men from the "better" families, lads who were always overspending their allowances in pursuit of pleasure. He discovered that farmers who raised horses and shipped them to New York often had difficulty getting reliable agents to handle their transactions. Many rogues gypped them on the sale price, or, if the deal was rewarding enough, simply absconded with the entire proceeds. Calling on the services of scions of the "best" families who were obligated to him through his moneylending, Sage got them to spread the word that he was just about the most honest and trustworthy person in existence. And so, at fifteen, buckskin-clad, the first fuzz of manhood sprouting on his cheeks, he was put in charge of a shipload of horses for delivery to the New York market. He disposed of the animals at a handsome profit, kept meticulous accounts, returned every penny to his employers—and was rewarded, so astonished were they, with a $700 bonus for his honesty, a fabulous windfall in days when the dollar was worth about seven or eight times what it is now.

This $700 nest egg enabled him to buy a half-interest in the Sage grocery when his brother Henry became too ill to carry on the business. The other half-share was purchased by another brother, Elisha Montague Sage, and before long the Sage Brothers store was booming as never before. Never content to have just one good thing going for him, Russell purchased a Hudson River sloop and, at nineteen, became a river captain, doing his own trading up and down the stream.

This experience led directly to his first great coup, one that became the foundation of his later fortune. In early November, 1836, the Hudson River froze solid from bank to bank. Several trading sloops were caught in the ice jam, and late produce from the countryside gathered on the wharves. Rivermen and farmers alike panicked.

Only Russell Sage did not panic. He studied weather records as far back as they went and discovered that this was the *only* time the Hudson had ever frozen over so early in the year. He reasoned from this that the cold spell was a fluke, that there would probably be a spell of milder weather before winter really set in—and therefore it was time to gamble.

To the horror of his brother Montague, he scraped up every available dollar and purchased three of the ice-bound sloops and tons of the produce on the wharves. Montague and virtually everyone else considered him mad, but the thaw Russell had anticipated came almost on schedule, and he sailed away downriver with his heavily laden vessels. In New York he disposed of the cargoes at such prices that he came out of the venture with a clear $50,000 profit, a sum probably equivalent to $350,000–$400,000 by today's values.

Russell Sage returned to Troy in triumph, went back to Durhamville for Thanksgiving, and paid off the mortgage on his parents' farm.

Russell was a handsome youth. Standing just under six feet in his seaboots, he carried himself so ramrod straight that he looked taller than he actually was. He had a curly brown beard that covered a square, determined chin; and he had—perhaps his most notable feature, the best clue to the inner man—steel-blue eyes, gimlet sharp.

There was now no stopping Russell Sage. The boy who had found ways to make a profit on a four-dollar-a-month income was now a young man with a fortune that could be used to build an ever greater fortune. In 1840, when he was only twenty-four, Sage was appointed to the Troy City Council. In the same year, he married Marie-Henrie

Winne, aged eighteen, daughter of Moses I. Winne, the local lumber king whose seat on the council he had taken. The boy from the poor Durhamville farm was now moving in ever more exclusive social circles. By the time he was thirty-two Sage was a power. He was president of the Troy City Council, treasurer of Rensselaer County, president of the Troy and Schenectady Railroad, and financial backer of Thurlow Weed, the Albany publisher who was later to become the Republican boss of the state.

Railroads were the new glamor industry of the time just as airplanes were to be a century later. They gave Sage the perfect opportunity to practice one of his favorite maxims: "Patriotism for profit." Only, with Sage and many others, the profit came first and the patriotism was purely incidental.

The city of Troy had invested $750,000 of public funds in the Troy and Schenectady Railroad, which had the only railroad bridge connecting the east bank of the Hudson with the west and Albany. Despite this advantage, the railroad was operating at a loss of $100,000 a year, and the city fathers became disenchanted. They concluded that they had a white elephant on their hands, and in their attempt to rid themselves of this incubus, they turned to the man with all the contacts—Russell Sage.

Sage had a three-way leverage. He was president of the council, president of the railroad, and one of the founders and directors of the New York Central, the Vanderbilt line that was becoming one of the most powerful in the nation. Playing all ends to his own advantage, Sage arranged a deal: he persuaded the Troy City Council to dispose of the Troy and Schenectady to a man who just happened to be a fellow director of the New York Central and his secret partner. The sale price for the $750,000 line was a mere $200,000; and, of this, only $50,000 was put down, the rest of the payment to be spread over fourteen years.

A bare four months after Sage and his partner had secured this bargain, they sold the Troy and Schenectady to their own New York Central for $780,000. Not only that, the Central was so grateful that Sage and his partner were awarded 6,500 shares of Central stock, valued at $120 a share. Sage's net profit from this bit of fancy wheeling and dealing was estimated at well over $1 million.

Though there were no conflict-of-interest laws barring a public official from dealing with his own firm for personal profit, one might have thought that the citizens of Troy would have realized they had been royally bilked. On the contrary, they were so grateful to Sage for the pocket-picking that had removed the burden of their supposed white elephant that they turned the other cheek and elected him to Congress.

Sage now became a lobbyist with portfolio. Usually the lobbyist has to bribe or influence a congressman to grant him special favors. But in this case, Sage *was* the congressman, able to use his official position to lobby for his own interests.

During his two terms in Congress he operated on two levels: he acquired control of a number of midwestern "railroads" that existed only on paper, and then he pushed through Congress a measure making millions of acres of public lands available as a gift to owners of just such "roads"—essentially to Sage himself and a few close associates.

Financial experts would later write that Sage and a collaborating lobbyist-promoter, John I. Blair of New Jersey, perfected the blueprint by which lobbyists of the period transferred millions of acres of the public domain to private pockets. They bribed public officials; they bought off the press; they assessed the weaknesses of influential men —and saw to it that these weaknesses were gratified. Blair's operations were confined to Iowa (though he later became associated with Sage in the scandal-tarred Union Pacific), but Sage, by far the more important figure of the two, cut a swath across both Wisconsin and Minnesota.

Sage had sensed the enormous wealth to be reaped from the rich, dark farmlands of Wisconsin during an early trip west in 1847, and he kept his covetous eyes on the Milwaukee and Mississippi franchise. When the original promoters failed to turn their paper railroad into iron rails, Sage gobbled up their franchise for a song. Then, in similar fashion, he acquired the character of another "paper" line, the La Crosse and Mississippi, which had been granted rights to lay rails from Lake Michigan to the great river. Two other rail lines that existed only on maps fell into Sage's hands, putting him in a position to reap a windfall if, in his capacity as a congressman, he could persuade the national legislature to grant him some rich favors.

This was a crucial era in which the great issues that were to produce the Civil War preoccupied both houses of Congress. Sage could not have been less interested. While the great free-soil versus slavery debates raged all around him, he chided his colleagues in speech after speech for devoting so much attention to an inconsequential topic. The important business facing the nation, he contended, was the construction of a railroad to the Pacific.

Sage never succeeded in convincing his colleagues that his pet railroad project was more important than the issues that were soon to tear the nation apart, but he did engineer through Congress a measure of inestimable value to himself—an act granting the state of Wisconsin 2,388,000 acres of public land that could then be distributed to railroad builders. To whom? To Sage, of course, the man who held all those paper-railroad charters.

Assured of this bonanza in real estate, Sage organized the machinery to kill the Wisconsin fatted calf. He established his "railroad" headquarters in an office at 23 William Street in downtown New York and gathered about him a number of prominent men who were to play large roles in some of the most reprehensible railroad finagling of the next decade. They included John A. Dix, who was to become a Civil War general and, later, president of the Union Pacific, and Samuel J. Tilden, an astute Democratic lawyer and reformer who was kept out of the presidency in 1876 only by a fraudulent count of Southern ballots.

Sage was the mastermind, the holder of all those paper-railroad franchises, and it was he who directed the campaign to buy the political influence necessary for the rip-off. In 1856 Sage's group issued what a select committee of the Wisconsin legislature later called $1 million worth of "corruption bonds." These bonds on Sage's paper-thin La Crosse and Milwaukee were then parceled out to thirteen state senators, seventy assemblymen, and a number of state officers. Governor Coles Bashford was rewarded with a $50,000 bundle, much to his later discomfiture.

Like any astute lobbyist, Sage did not overlook the vital necessity of molding public opinion. Whenever big private interests are to be served, it is always a wise precaution to ensure the slumbering disinterest of a potentially nosy press—and so another $246,000 worth of Sage's "corruption bonds" were bestowed upon susceptible newspaper editors and molders of public opinion. As a consequence, all potential opposition, official and private, was conveniently silenced and nobody was looking when the Wisconsin legislature obligingly gave Sage's "paper" railroad land grants later estimated to be worth $17 million. In effect, Sage had translated a virtual zero into millions. His $1 million worth of fancily engraved corporate paper represented for him only out-of-pocket printing costs, but he had used it to corrupt the leaders of an entire state and had walked off with a veritable gold mine in real estate. Having lobbied himself into the makings of a vast fortune, he now donned his other hat, that of corporate tycoon, and employed every artifice of financial skullduggery to rip off stockholders in his own companies for the benefit of himself and his small coterie of insiders.

With the land grant financing the future, Sage now organized a construction company to build the railroad. This, naturally, was no ordinary construction company, as it was owned by the insiders who were pulling all the wires from 23 William Street. This cozy dual relationship was made to order for barely legal larceny. With the insiders dictating every move, each mile of track was laid at double or triple the legitimate cost, a procedure that picked the pockets of the railroad's stockholders as it siphoned off every available dollar into the coffers of the construction company—and the insiders.

When the swindle became too odorous for even the clogged nostrils of that insensitive era, the Wisconsin legislature launched its belated investigation, and several things happened. Governor Bashford, in panic, dumped his $50,000 worth of bonds for $15,000 and departed hastily for Arizona. And Sage and his colleagues shuffled corporate papers. With the La Crosse and Milwaukee having served its purpose, they organized the Minnesota and Milwaukee, sequestering all their own assets under the new corporate shelter. The process was repeated again and again, with ordinary stockholders being fleeced at every step and the insiders reaping enormous profits.

Wisconsin was little more than an appetizer in a full-course meal. Beyond Wisconsin lay Minnesota, and the Sage group organized the Minnesota and Pacific with the promise to "open up the primitive Northwest." They were going to extend rails all the way to the Pacific, they proclaimed. Naturally, as a reward for this patriotic enterprise, they expected certain favors. The state of Minnesota almost fell over itself to oblige. Sage's combine was given 14 million acres of the state's best timber and farmland, and was showered with subsidies and tax exemptions.

Incredibly, these bounties were not enough to keep the poor old Minnesota and Pacific afloat. The insiders looted the till, plunged the railroad into bankruptcy, and then, just as they had done in Wisconsin, they transferred control to a new corporate front, the St. Paul and Pacific. In the process, Sage managed to squirrel out for his own personal portfolio thirty thousand acres of the richest farmland in Stearns County, a barony from which he reaped a rich harvest for nearly fifty years.

Victimized stockholders were naturally enraged, but when they sought justice in the courts, their cases came before federal judge John F. Dillon in St. Paul, and Dillon, as later events demonstrated, was virtually in Sage's hip pocket. He never failed to rule in Sage's favor, and it was hardly a coincidence that, when he retired from the federal bench, he became the well-paid counsel for Sage and Jay Gould, by this time powers in the Union Pacific.

The tactics of Sage and his coterie now seem so familiar that they might have been copied from a textbook on lobbying. Governor William Larrabee of Iowa later described the myriad methods by which they achieved and maintained such overwhelming influence. They first determined "the weakness and wants of every man whose services they were likely to need." Corporate support was given rising politicians; hungry lawyers were put on the corporate payroll; vain men were flattered with newspaper publicity. Favorite shippers were granted advantageous rates over their competitors, and lesser lights were wooed with passes giving them and their families free-riding privileges. Such measures guaranteed support and muted opposition.

Sage's operations in Wisconsin and Minnesota were only a prelude to the greatest swindle of all, the building of the famed Union Pacific. As a congressman, Sage had not been able to secure passage of his Pacific Railroad bill, but the Civil War placed new emphasis on the importance of rail transportation and made the building of a rail network to the Pacific seem like a patriotic enterprise. As a result, Congress in 1862 passed the Pacific Railroad Act. To implement it, a charter was issued to the Union Pacific to lay track westward from Nebraska; and another, to the Central Pacific to work eastward from California.

Congress attempted to maintain control over the Union Pacific through a cumbersome board composed of 5 government representatives and 158 commissioners appointed from the various states and territories. This ruling body was supposed to elect the railroad's officers and sponsor a $100 million stock offering to the public. But not even Congress could control the Wall Street buccaneers who sniffed in the Union Pacific the aroma of the juiciest melon they would ever have the opportunity to slice.

Less than a year after Congress thought it had established public control of the new railroad, a group of financial moguls met quietly in New York and booted government representatives right off the controlling board. By this act, which drew not a murmur of protest from a complaisant Congress, they established the Union Pacific as a private, independent enterprise, ripe for plucking. Among those participating in this corporate coup were two longtime associates of Sage, Samuel J. Tilden and John A. Dix; the American agent of the Rothschild banking interests, August Belmont, himself a man of great wealth; Leonard W. Jerome, millionaire stockbroker and future grandfather of British Prime Minister Winston Churchill; Thurlow Weed, the New York State Republican boss whom Sage had helped to finance; and Thomas C. Durant, a former physician who had taken up railroad promotion and had been involved in the bungled affairs of three lesser lines.

Durant was one of the largest stockholders and soon became the major power on the Union Pacific board. It was he who brought into the act an eccentric genius who was one of the wiliest and most flamboyant lobbyists the nation has ever known—George Francis Train.

Train was born in Boston on March 24, 1829. Like Sage, he went to work as a young boy, and before he was twenty-one he had laid the foundation for his future fortune. He began working in the Boston shipping firm of his uncle, Enoch Train, when he was fifteen, and he was so industrious, with such a sure promoter's instinct, that he had a share in the business worth $10,000 a year by the time he was twenty.

His was a mind always attuned to gambling on new developments, and so he immediately recognized the significance of the discovery of gold in California in 1848. At his urging, the Train firm built a fleet of forty clipper ships to carry gold-seekers and their equipment around Cape Horn. Among these vessels was the famous *Flying Cloud*, queen of clippers in her day, designed and built by Donald McKay especially for the Train interests.

When gold was discovered in Australia a few years later, Train found his office job in Boston too boring and joined the new gold rush. In Australia he established a shipping and commission business that soon was netting him $95,000 a year. This was the beginning of his global wanderings. When he tired of Australia, he moved on to India, wrote a book about his Australian experiences, and finally wound up in Paris, where he became a dashing figure in court circles and the intimate of Emperor Louis Napoleon and Empress Eugénie. His French sojourn was to be important in his later career, for it was here that he observed the operations of a corporate device on which he was later to pattern the scandal-ridden Crédit Mobilier.

Train was a tall, handsome man with a dark complexion and a

great shock of curly hair that, in later life, receded and turned snow white. He had a wide, flowing mustache and the kind of hail-fellow personality a promoter needs, one that made an impression on all kinds and classes of people from common folk to crowned heads. On one visit to Madrid, he so charmed Queen María Cristina that she invested a sizable fortune in the so-called Atlantic and Great Western Railroad, one of the worst frauds of this fraudulent era. The company was soon absorbed into the Erie, and insiders were lining their pockets with the stockholders' money, including the investment of Queen Cristina.

The man who could bamboozle a queen was just the man needed to bamboozle the great American public. Dr. Thomas Durant, a kindred spirit, had come to admire Train's talents during previous rail manipulations, and now he decided to call Train home from London, where Train had established the first British street railway lines. Almost at once, Train became a matchless drumbeater for the infant Union Pacific. His florid style of oratory and his persuasive manner aroused the patriotic fervor of cowhands and charmed legislators. He was the ideal front man, and for several years, to the public at large, he *was* the Union Pacific.

The kind of rhetoric he used to wrap the railroad in the folds of the flag is perhaps best illustrated by a speech he made on December 2, 1863, during groundbreaking ceremonies for the eastern terminus of the line in what was then the tiny prairie village of Omaha, Nebraska.

"Before the first century of the nation's birth," he proclaimed, "we may see in the New York depot some strange Pacific railway notice: 'European passengers for Japan will please take the night train. Passengers for China this way.'"

He roared on, linking railroad and nation in a brotherhood of destiny:

"The Pacific Railroad is the nation, and the nation is the Pacific Railroad. Labor and capital shake hands today. The two united make the era of progress. Congress gives something toward building this great natural thoroughfare—not much, but something; say a loan of government credit for thirty years for $16,000 a mile and 20,000,000 acres of land. But what is that in these times?"

Obviously, a mere bagatelle, for Train's imagination soared to yet more fevered heights in this prediction: "Ten millions of immigrants will settle in this golden land in twenty years."

Only a skinflint or someone too myopic to catch the patriotic vision could possibly balk at the governmental giveaways that were to do so much for those "ten millions of immigrants" and those passengers entraining for China and Japan. Certainly members of Congress did not wish to be so stigmatized, and they therefore opened wide the national pocketbook. They granted the Union Pacific subsidies varying from $16,000 to $48,000 a mile for laying track, the difference depending upon the difficulties of the terrain. In addition, they donated to the road 12 million acres of public land. State legislatures were equally generous, with Nebraska, as one observer commented, giving the Union Pacific "nearly every power imaginable, save that of reconstructing the late rebel states."

Train, like Sage before him, took advantage of this real estate handout to reserve for his personal benefit 5,000 lots in what was to become the city of Omaha. Having helped himself in this fashion, Train next devised the scheme that was to enrich the Union Pacific's insiders and rock the national government with a scandal that still reeks in the history books. This was his creation of Crédit Mobilier.

While poring through the Pennsylvania archives, Train discovered that a charter had been issued in 1859 to an obscure company known as the Pennsylvania Fiscal Agency. What intrigued Train was the broad sweep of power granted the company. It could engage in virtually any enterprise except banking. Despite this unlimited franchise, the so-called fiscal agency had been a fiscal flop, and Train was able to purchase its charter for $25,000. Then, with a little subtle bribery, he induced the Pennsylvania legislature to change the name to Crédit Mobilier of America.

The idea harked back to Train's experiences in France. He had been impressed by the success of Emile and Isaac Pereire, two brothers who operated the Société Générale de Crédit Mobilier. Their company had been organized to make loans on personal or mobile property, but the Pereire brothers had used the charter to branch out into brokerage and banking—and so had become dominant figures in the French financial world.

Train's Crédit Mobilier, like its French model, had the power to do almost anything short of declaring war. Durant, who had made himself president of Union Pacific, was so enchanted with the possibilities for wholesale larceny that, in a burst of generosity, he rewarded Train with a $25,000 bonus and another $25,000 worth of Crédit Mobilier stock. Soon more of Crédit Mobilier's fancy paper was finding its way into the grasping hands of some of the most important politicians in Washington, men in a position to do the Union Pacific an infinite amount of good.

In 1864 Train, lobbying furiously, pushed through Congress an amended Pacific Railroad Act that doubled the Union Pacific's land grant to 24 million acres and reinforced the government's underwriting of its securities. The deed was done despite the protests of Representative Elihu B. Washbourne of Illinois, the close friend of Abraham Lincoln. Washbourne called the new land grab "the greatest legislative crime in history."

Even while Washbourne was crying out that the U.S. Treasury was going to be looted for $95 million, the insiders began to ladle out the gravy. Durant, deciding that Train had served his purpose, elbowed him aside, and the colorful promoter went off to Omaha to develop his free-gift real estate and proclaim himself founder of the city. Not liking his hotel accommodations, he protested, and the arrogant proprietor unwisely told him that if he didn't like it, he should go and build himself his own hotel. The taunt was all Train needed. In just sixty days, he built a new hotel—and named it the Cozzens after the landlord who had mocked him.

While Train was so preoccupied in Omaha, Durant and his associates began the looting of the Union Pacific, using Train's brainchild, Crédit Mobilier. The Union Pacific's chief engineer estimated that the first hundred miles of track could be laid for $30,000 a mile, but Crédit Mobilier was given the job at double that price.

The total swag could never be accurately computed. The version generally accepted for years was that the laying of the Union Pacific line from Omaha to Promontory Point in Utah, where it joined with the Central Pacific coming east, should have cost some $50 million instead of the $94 million paid on corrupt contracts. Later reassessments have whittled down this estimated $44 million boodle to between $13 million and $16.5 million, still monumental larceny in the days of the uninflated dollar.

The booty was, indeed, so immense that, as often happens, the thieves fell out in a quarrel over the spoils. And when this occurred, the whole Crédit Mobilier scandal blew like the first spout from a new oil well. The prelude to the explosion came in December, 1867, when Crédit Mobilier declared its first dividend—an incredibly rewarding 100 percent. A month later came the rupture.

The insiders, meeting in early January, 1868, had a problem: only 650 shares of Crédit Mobilier stock were left to be distributed, and there were three claimants—Thomas Durant, Congressman Oakes Ames, and Henry S. McComb, of Wilmington, Delaware. Both Durant and Ames argued that they had promised stock to members of Congress, and these commitments, they said, must be honored. McComb, who had been involved in Civil War contract scandals, insisted that 375 shares had been promised to him three years earlier. No one could remember such a promise, and Sidney Dillon, president of Crédit Mobilier, excoriated McComb in righteous tones that, considering the company, had an almost ludicrous ring to them. McComb, said Dillon, had advanced a claim "so base and fraudulent that, in presenting it, he had shown himself to be a scoundrel unworthy to associate with gentlemen."

The self-styled "gentlemen" thereupon rejected McComb's claim and split the remaining stock between Ames and Durant. McComb, furious, stalked out of the meeting, muttering threats, but the "gentlemen" shrugged their shoulders and laughed them off. McComb, they thought, couldn't be serious.

That was where they were wrong. McComb, a vindictive man, nursed his grudge for three years, then filed suit against Crédit Mobilier in Pennsylvania. In support of his claim, he introduced letters from Oakes Ames, who had indiscreetly mentioned placing Crédit Mobilier shares among members of Congress, "where they will do the most good." Ames had compounded this indiscretion by sending McComb the names of a number of congressmen who might fall into the "most good" category.

These explosive charges in the court record did not cause the instantaneous eruption one might have expected, but in September, 1872, as President Grant was running for reelection, the New York *Sun* let loose a blast under the glaring headline: THE KING OF FRAUDS: HOW THE CREDIT MOBILIER BOUGHT ITS WAY INTO CONGRESS.

Grant, the hero general of the Civil War, was reelected, of course, but Congress, when it reconvened in December, 1872, found itself so suspect in the public mind that it was under the embarrassing necessity of having to do something. So great was the pressure that two of the most prominent names on the alleged bribery list—Speaker of the House James G. Blaine and Representative James A. Garfield of Ohio, later to become the twentieth President—moved for a full-scale investigation.

The nation was then treated to the spectacle of the accused investigating themselves—and turning and twisting in evasive maneuvers as they sought to bring about a whitewash that would not look like a whitewash. Blaine, who was beholden to many railroad interests, especially those of Jay Cooke's Northern Pacific, was in the clear in the Crédit Mobilier case because he had not accepted ten shares of stock as had been charged.

Garfield was less fortunate. He declared under oath that he had never received a share of Crédit Mobilier stock or accepted a dividend. The evidence showed otherwise, but the committee was anxious to exonerate. As Claude G. Bowers later wrote in *The Tragic Era:* "The committee was to find that he [Garfield] had owned stock, did receive a dividend, and had perjured himself—and was therefore innocent."

The vice-presidents in Grant's two administrations fared little better. Schuyler Colfax, the vice-president in the first administration, was one of the most sanctimonious of men. He had made a great parade of his Christian virtues during the fall campaign and had denied under oath that he had had any ties with Crédit Mobilier. Unfortunately for him, Oakes Ames had kept a memorandum book, and one entry showed that Colfax had received a $1,200 dividend check. This disclosure sent Colfax into silent hibernation for days, but then he came up with an explanation. Practically all of that $1,200, which undeniably he had received, had been forwarded to him as "a political gift" by a longtime friend and admirer who, as luck would have it, was now dead. It was too much for even this partisan investigating committee. The committee decided that Colfax had sworn falsely, and Colfax's presidential ambitions died with the finding.

Vice-president Henry Wilson, who succeeded Colfax in the second Grant administration, was also involved in the scandal as the willing recipient of Crédit Mobilier favors, but the committee decided he had not been corrupt, merely indiscreet. And so he continued in his high office and presided over the Senate.

A number of congressmen who had had no defense were similarly adjudged to have been naive and unwise, but not corrupt or evil. However, since indisputably there had been a lot of corruption, such findings produced an inevitable dilemma: *somebody* must have done *something* wrong, and so it was essential to find some scapegoats who could be offered as sacrifices to an indignant public. As often happens in such cases, the whitewashers of important official reputations selected as the prime villain the one man who had testified honestly—Oakes Ames. Ames had committed the cardinal sin of turning state's evidence and testifying against fellow congressmen, and the investigating committee of his peers trumpeted righteously that he and another member, Representative James Brooks of New York, ought to be drummed right out of the club. The expulsion resolution was eventually watered down to a simple vote of censure, but both Ames and Brooks were ruined men.

Disillusioned by the unabashed perjury and knavery of his colleagues, the shaken Oakes Ames wondered at one point whether he was the only truthful man in the whole House.

Such was the upheaval produced by the Crédit Mobilier brainchild of George Francis Train. Though Train himself had had no part in the final buying of congressmen, the corporate vehicle he had devised had been used by insiders first to swindle the railroad stockholders, then to corrupt public officials on a wholesale scale. In the process, it had produced the worst scandal in the nation's history prior to the Teapot Dome disclosures of the early 1920s.

The late 1850s saw the birth of lobbying on the massive scale that has been a familiar feature of the Washington scene ever since. The nation had suffered one of its worst economic disasters in the panic of 1857. As banks crashed, businesses failed, and stocks became virtually worthless, the losers in every segment of society sent their agents scurrying to the nation's capital in search of resuscitation and sustenance.

The railroad lobbyists, who had already been tilling the fertile fields of federal influence, were now joined by a horde of self-seekers representing manufacturers, bankers, brokers, real estate interests, and speculators of every stripe, all anxious to share in the bonanzas bequeathed by an Uncle Sam turned Santa Claus.

Congress was flooded with giveaway bills: schemes for the appropriation of public lands, proposals to strip the Indians of all their remaining holdings, a "homestead bill" to give a farm to everyone who asked, and appeals for funds and ever more funds to widen rivers, deepen harbors, and build lighthouses, docks and customhouses, post offices and barracks, hospitals and subtreasury buildings.

The lobbyists who competed for these various plums were a scurvy lot. No form of skullduggery was repugnant to them. Blackmail was a favorite device.

Washington was a wide-open city, cluttered with gambling houses whose proprietors often fronted for the lobbyists. Once this unscrupulous gambler-lobbyist partnership got a congressman or senator in debt at the gaming tables, the squeeze was put on. The gambler would insist on

SAM WARD, KING OF THE LOBBY

full payment, which was often impossible, or in the event the legislator could get together the cash, exposure would be threatened. Trapped, the hapless lawmaker had only one avenue of escape—to vote as he was told on a particular measure dear to the lobbyist hidden behind the menacing figure of the crook.

Into this immortal atmosphere there now stepped one of the most unusual lobbyists in history, a man of brilliance and charm, with the intelligence of a genius and the foibles of a playboy. He was Samuel Ward, intellectual, connoisseur of wines, women, and high living; a spendthrift who ran through several fortunes as fast as he accumulated them; a sartorial fashion-plate, the most genial of hosts, a witty raconteur whose personality charmed virtually everyone he met.

Ward's qualities have been summed up best by his principal biographer, Lately Thomas, who called him a "beaming apostle of good cheer who seemed to have traveled everywhere and known everybody —who conversed like an angel, was a man of distinguished comportment in any society—who discussed business with bankers, theology with divines, equations with mathematicians, literature with authors, music with virtuosi, all with equal fluency and authority—who sparkled with backstage anecdotes when among actors and swapped wilderness adventures when among explorers—who saluted ladies with bouquets and verses, recited Horace and Homer, told a gay story with an irresistible twinkle, and when among *bons vivants* dilated upon vintages and chefs in masterly fashion."

Sam Ward was born into his first fortune on January 27, 1814, in a small, boxlike house near New York's Battery Park. His father, also named Samuel, was a banker and a partner in the prominent Wall Street firm of Prime and Ward.

The Ward family's roots went far back into American history, to the seventeenth century. Thomas Ward, a captain in Oliver Cromwell's cavalry, had emigrated to America when Charles II regained the English throne. Two of his descendants became governors of Rhode Island. The second of these, the first Samuel Ward, was little Sam's great-grandfather. Governor Ward was the only chief executive in the colonies to oppose the hated Stamp Act, and he became a delegate to both the First and Second Continental Congresses, helping to lay the groundwork for the Declaration of Independence.

Young Sam's grandfather was Lieutenant Colonel Samuel Ward, who had fought in the Continental Army during the Revolution all the way from the early attack on Quebec to the final surrender of British forces at Yorktown. After the war the colonel moved to New York and established a mercantile business that became the foundation of the family fortune. In 1788 he sailed to Canton, becoming one of the first Americans to visit the Far East. In the course of a long life he fathered ten children, seven of whom (two daughters and five sons) lived to maturity. The males of the family all stood more than six feet tall and were ruggedly built.

The boy who was to become the most famous lobbyist of his day was of shorter and slighter stature. Portraits of him in his youth show a slender, dapper young man with a mass of light brown curly hair, and a dark mustache and goatee on a narrow-planed face. The nose was long and straight, and wide-spaced, brilliant dark eyes that sparkled like diamonds were set under high-arched brows. With age, the face would become full and round, the mustache and flowing beard snow white; the slender figure would succumb to an impressive, protruding paunch; and the hair would disappear except for a sparse white fringe above the ears.

Sam's mother, married at sixteen, died of tuberculosis when only twenty-seven, but not before she had given birth to three sons and three daughters. One of the daughters, always young Sam's favorite in the family, was to become Julia Ward Howe, famed for writing "The Battle Hymn of the Republic." Another, Louisa, would marry one of the foremost sculptors of the day, Thomas Crawford, who fashioned the Armed Liberty atop the illuminated Capitol dome in Washington. It was a remarkable family, and Sam was undoubtedly the most remarkable member of it.

He had a mind that soaked up knowledge like a sponge. Higher mathematics were for him as easy as simple arithmetic. Languages he absorbed as easily as breathing. He could quote verbatim whole passages from Horace. He dabbled in poetry and often expressed a desire to devote himself to "the muse"—but other matters always came up to claim his attention. Singleness of purpose was not for him.

Sam was destined ultimately to enter his family's banking business, but he struggled against this fate as long as he could. He went to Europe to finish his education, and there, a young man barely twenty, he began to exhibit those traits that were to be both his cross and his charm. He devoted himself at first to serious study, but soon immersed himself in the social whirl, gallivanting from city to city, enjoying himself hugely everywhere he went. He was irresponsible with money.

Back home, his staid banker father tried to limit his expenditures, but Sam, drawing on his father's London bankers, always spent more than he had. He became an authority on the best foods, the best wines, the most attractive women. His conversation sparkled, and he drew friends like a magnet. One of these, a man who was to become a lifelong friend, was Henry Wadsworth Longfellow, the famous early-American poet.

This gay and carefree life, intermixed with a variety of intellectual pursuits, came to an end in the fall of 1836, when Sam could no longer put off the inevitable: the necessity of returning home and becoming a banker. He hated it. He loved to spend money in prodigious quantities, but he detested slogging over ledgers to get the money to spend. Romance helped relieve his boredom. A highly eligible young bachelor in the social whirl of New York, he met and married Emily Astor, the granddaughter of the first fabulously wealthy American, John Jacob Astor. Sam's father, happy to see him settling down, gave the new couple a spacious house at 32 Bond Street, and in time Emily gave birth to a daughter whom Sam adored and about whom he wrote ecstatic letters to Longfellow.

But fate seemed to have decreed that Sam Ward was never to lead a settled life. Tragedies came swiftly, one piled upon another. Sam's father died in 1839. In February, 1841, Emily gave birth to a second child, a boy. At first all seemed well, but then an infection set in and, in a matter of days, both mother and son were dead. "I am heartbroken," Sam wrote Longfellow.

The next years were filled with many activities that had nothing to do with banking. Sam lectured before the Mercantile Library Association, sharing the season's program with other, already famous speakers—Longfellow, essayist Ralph Waldo Emerson, and educator Horace Mann. He spent many weekends traveling to Boston to be with Longfellow, and he became a kind of literary agent for the poet, haunting New York editors to get the best prices for the work of his friend. He went further: out of his own vast reading, he culled themes and suggested ideas, some of which Longfellow turned into effective poetry.

It was not to be expected that so mercurial a widower would remain single forever, but Sam's choice of a second mate dismayed his family, alienated the Astors, and was frowned upon by New York society. The girl was Medora Grymes, a vivid Louisianian and the most dazzling beauty to descend upon the city in years. Her fortune-hunting mother, Suzette, who was alienated from her playboy husband, John

Randolph Grymes, had come to New York determined to marry Medora to wealth, and the first wealth she chose was that of an aging Frenchman. Sam Ward, however, was a millionaire, young, personable, engaging; and the engagement to the Frenchman was broken. Medora and Sam were married on September 20, 1843. It was a union of two spoiled, unstable characters, and, predictably, disaster followed.

There was the usual honeymoon euphoria, but Sam's bliss with Medora was not destined to endure. Sam was basically a gambler, playing for the highest stakes in the hope of obtaining quickly all the millions he could ever squander, a fortune large enough to free him from banking and let him devote himself to his intellectual loves—mathematics, poetry, the arts. His recklessness alienated the older and more conservative members of the banking firm, and the result was almost inevitable. In September, 1847, Sam's firm crashed in a failure that shook Wall Street.

His marriage, though it tottered along for a time, virtually crashed with the firm. A vast fortune was needed to keep Medora in the spoiled life-style to which she had become accustomed—and Sam no longer had a fortune. In an effort to get another, he left his wife and their two young sons with his cawing mother-in-law and went off to the newly discovered gold fields of California.

The magic of his personality won him instant friends and influence in the brawling life of San Francisco. Before embarking for California, Sam had figured out that the fastest and easiest way to fortune lay, not in wading knee-deep in streams to pan gold, but in supplying a raw frontier with the manufactured articles it needed. And so he set up a commission business—and soon was rich again. Within a few months, he estimated he was worth some $250,000, the equivalent of being a millionaire today.

This fortune, like others he was to accumulate in his long and active life, quickly vanished. A disastrous fire swept San Francisco, wiping out his business. He was again almost without a dollar and reduced to scrounging for a new grubstake. Medora, never one to accept adversity, had gone off to Paris with her mother and by all accounts was soon living the life of a courtesan. There would follow in the years to come, during those times when Sam had money, brief periods of happiness and reconciliation, but nothing would last. Sam was separated from his children: the Astors had custody of his daughter and turned her mind against him; Medora had his two sons with her in Europe. Alone, almost without resources, Sam Ward began to live the febrile life of a man who depended solely on his wit and charm and personality—he became a lobbyist.

Ward's first ventures in this new field remain clouded in the mists of intrigue. In 1854 one of Sam's San Francisco friends, the French Count Raousset-Boulbon, headed an expedition into Mexico to carve out an independent republic of Sonora, with the object of taking over the long-abandoned Sonora gold and silver mines, among the richest in the world. The invaders were overwhelmed and captured, and the cruel, treacherous dictator of Mexico, Antonio López de Santa Anna, vowed he would execute them all.

Californians were shocked. A large sum of money was raised to ransom the prisoners. Sam Ward, with his gift of languages and his courtly manners, was chosen as the emissary to deal with Santa Anna. Sam went to Mexico City, where he adopted the lobbying practices he was later to use so skillfully in Washington: he courted favor subtly by lavish entertaining. He played host to leading politicians and diplomats. His dinners were elaborate, the best wines sparkling, the courses so expertly prepared they would make the mouth of a gourmet water. The wives of the influential and powerful were showered with bouquets and attentions, and when Sam organized a dancing class to teach them the steps that were the latest rage in Paris, he became famous, and his conquest of the feminine community was almost complete.

With the entire upper strata of society virtually in the palm of his hand, Sam Ward gradually cultivated the vain and capricious Santa Anna. Just how much money was passed under the table and how it was arranged, no one will ever know, but the results were obvious. Raousset was executed before Sam had a chance to save him, but Santa Anna freed the remaining prisoners.

Sam's success in placating the implacable dictator impressed foreign businessmen in Mexico City, and Sam left the capital mysteriously bankrolled by international commercial interests. He was dispatched on a mission to Europe, the exact nature of which remains a mystery. Apparently he served as some kind of link between European investors and business agents in America, an employment that gave Sam a sudden, if temporary, burst of affluence.

Naturally, being Sam, he spent money as if there were no tomorrow. He toured Europe, renewing old friendships and acquaintances, and making new. Among the latter was one of the most famous novelists of the day, William Makepeace Thackeray, author of *Vanity*

Fair and *Henry Esmond.* Thackeray was then in Paris, finishing *The Newcomes,* and he rapidly became as fond of Sam as Longfellow had always been.

The wining and dining in the most expensive restaurants, the traveling and sightseeing, the expensive gifts to friends, all a fixed pattern of life with incorrigible Sam, led to the inevitable end—an empty purse. Back in America in the fall of 1858, Sam was so broke that he appealed desperately to Longfellow for a loan and received $250, all the poet could spare. Then, just as his fortunes were at their lowest ebb, Sam grabbed an official lifeline, a $1,500 annual salary from the federal government as secretary and interpreter for a diplomatic mission to Paraguay.

A dispute with Paraguay had been simmering for years. Essentially, it involved a head-on collision between dictator Carlos Antonio López and a group of Rhode Island investors who had envisioned personal profits in bringing the benefits of modern industry to backward Paraguay. Edward Augustus Hopkins, a hotheaded former midshipman in the American navy, represented the investors; but when, in a fit of anger, he stormed into the presidential palace in muddy boots, waving a riding crop, López threw him out of the country and revoked his group's business charter. Subsequently, a Paraguayan fort fired on an American steamer, smashing one of her paddlewheels and killing the helmsman. The mission to which Sam Ward was attached was instructed to seek compensation for both offenses.

The expedition went in force—a fleet consisting of two frigates, two sloops-of-war, three brigs, and nine armed steamers, plus store ships. The warships mounted some two hundred guns and carried twenty-five hundred sailors and marines—a display of force sufficient to make even a dictator blink and think twice.

All the evidence indicates that Sam Ward now began to play a devious, double role. He was the only member of the mission who had a full, working knowledge of Spanish. So it seems most curious that, while the fleet was anchored off Buenos Aires in Argentina, a full set of the official instructions to Commissioner James B. Bowlin was written out in Spanish and smuggled to López. Bowlin was to demand $1 million compensation for the Rhode Island investors, but he had been authorized to cut this amount in half if necessary to achieve a settlement—certainly a handy bit of knowledge for López to have before the bargaining even began.

With persuasive Sam Ward playing a key role in the negotiations (after all, he was the only one who could communicate directly with López in Spanish), a settlement was reached that was quite painless to the dictator. López signed a new treaty of friendship and commerce with the United States, he agreed to pay $10,000 to the heirs of the slain helmsman, and he offered the Rhode Island investors $250,000, take it or leave it. In case this sum was rejected, López pledged himself to abide by whatever decision an arbitration commission might reach.

Commissioner Bowlin was allowed to believe he had scored a diplomatic triumph, but there were only two big winners in this deal: López and Sam Ward. When Sam returned to the fleet, he was sporting a ring with a brilliant sapphire that no one recalled having seen before, and he had to his credit a cash payment of one thousand pounds sterling, a princely reward from López for services rendered and others anticipated. In effect, at the same time that Sam held an official position in the American delegation, he had become an agent for the very dictator with whom the Americans were dealing.

Sam's role as lobbyist for López had to be kept secret, and so the two conspirators adopted code names. López became Nicolás Pérez, while Sam Ward was transformed into plain Pedro Fernandez. Their arrangement provided that Sam was to lobby for the swift passage of the new trade and arbitration agreements by the U.S. Senate; and when the case came to arbitration, Sam was to receive a bonus of two cents for every dollar sliced off the American rock-bottom figure of $500,000.

Sam Ward had found a good thing, and he lost no time taking advantage of it. Even before the fleet left Buenos Aires for home, poor Pedro Fernandez was informing Nicolás Pérez that he was hard pressed for money and would appreciate being paid one hundred pounds a month until the arbitration commission met. Pérez, wishing to keep this valuable ally inside the ranks of the opposition, was happy to oblige.

With the dictator's money, Sam Ward was once more in the chips and enjoying life. He made another trip to Europe, had another rendezvous with Thackeray in London, and met William Howard Russell, the world's first war correspondent, a journalist who was soon to accompany Sam in a historic tour of the South at the outbreak of the Civil War.

This European jaunt did not distract Sam from his major mission—looking out for the interests of Dictator López. Back in Washington, he was infinitely amused when an attorney for the complaining investors proposed that *he* become the American member of the arbitration commission. The lawyer wanted Sam to run up the charges against Paraguay, unaware that López had already hired him to keep the award down. Chuckling to himself, Sam declined the honor, content to be named secretary and interpreter for the arbitrators.

At the arbitration hearing, the attorney for the American investors demanded $1 million; the Paraguayan attorney, a capable lawyer whom Sam had recommended, argued that the investors weren't entitled to a cent because they had risked next to nothing in their grandiose projects and their claims were "inflated, fictitious and worthless." The evidence seemed to bear out this contention, and even the American member of the commission, Judge Cave Johnson, of Kentucky, decided that the investors had no legitimate claim.

President James Buchanan was outraged. He almost wept with vexation as he recalled that López had acknowledged to Bowlin the basic justice of the claim. All that was supposed to be settled was the amount. Sam Ward, dining with the President in the White House, was suave and sympathetic. He agreed it was a surprising, even shocking decision, but even as he spoke these soothing words, he was luxuriating in his private bonus of some $10,000 from López because the American bedrock figure of $500,000 had been whittled down to zero.

Altogether, Sam had collected some $18,000 from López in less than two years, in addition to extra fees and perquisites. This windfall enabled him to blossom forth in sartorial splendor—in brilliant cravats, spotless linen, diamond studs, rings on both hands, and always a rose in his lapel. He rented a house at 258 F Street and began to entertain lavishly. In a letter to his favorite sister, Julia Ward Howe, he chortled joyously: "I have my own crockery and set of silver marked S.W., which I earned by the sweat of my brow and the oil of my tongue."

One might question how much "sweat" had been involved, but there was no doubt about the "oil" of Sam's tongue. It was now 1860, and Sam Ward was the most sophisticated lobbyist in Washington. Such crudities as blackmailing a legislator over gambling debts were not for him. He relied on his role as genial host to all the important people. His weapons were his gourmet-laden table, the sparkle of his conversation, the shine of his personality. His was a charm that few could resist, and it was not long before he was on intimate terms with everyone who amounted to anything in the official life of Washington.

These contacts enabled him to swing business deals with the government to the immense profit of himself and his clients. Typical was a shadowy transaction mentioned in June, 1860, in letters to his friend, the wealthy New York lawyer S. L. M. Barlow. Ward and Barlow evidently were agents for the owners of a piece of property that was being sold to the federal government for $150,000. In a hastily scrawled note marked *Private,* Sam wrote Barlow: "I've got our affair so near you had better draw up the papers so there can be no mistake . . . I think we can allow them [the owners] $110,000—and of the balance $15,000 apiece for us and $10,000 for other purposes and parties." With the caution necessary for one engaging in such questionable deals, Sam did not spell out in writing just what he meant by "other purposes and parties," but it does not take much imagination to suggest that extra $10,000 was intended to grease some helpful palms.

★

With the outbreak of the Civil War, Sam's activity entered a new phase. One of his well-cultivated contacts in Washington was William H. Seward, secretary of state in the new administration of President Abraham Lincoln. Sam had many family connections and friends in the South, and he early formed the habit of passing on to Seward whatever information he gleaned from them.

Seward, who had expected to get the Republican nomination for President instead of Lincoln and who still deceived himself that he could steer Lincoln's course, could not believe that the South would secede from the Union. He deluded himself with the belief that strong Union sentiment existed in many of the southern states, and Sam, knowing this was not so, fought a long and indecisive battle to make Seward see the reality.

When William Howard Russell, the British war correspondent, arrived in New York on March 16, 1861, one of the first visitors to pop up at his hotel was Sam Ward. "That wonderful Sam Ward!" Russell wrote in his notebook. "I was trying to recall a line from Dante, when in walked Sam, and gave me the line straight from his memory, and half a dozen others, too."

Sam helped to open official doors for Russell, and he soon conceived the ambitious plan of touring the southern states in Russell's company to find out what was happening there. As a result, he was in Charleston, South Carolina, on April 12, 1861, when the Confederates opened fire on Fort Sumter and compelled its surrender, the act that precipitated the Civil War.

Russell joined Sam in Charleston, and the pair were well received in both social and military circles. As a result, Sam gathered a vast amount of useful information, which he sent back to the North in the same pouch that carried Russell's news dispatches to the London *Times*. Sam's communications were addressed to George Ellis Baker, a longtime follower and trusted aide of Seward, and they were signed "Charles Lopez," a name reminiscent of Sam's Paraguayan intrigues. Fortunately for Sam, Russell's "cover" as a war correspondent kept these dispatches from being discovered, for had they been, Sam Ward could very easily have been tried and shot as a spy.

In one communiqué that Baker forwarded to Seward, Sam warned, "While you are planning, these people are acting." He found a South united in rebellion, with Union sentiment virtually nonexistent, and he forecast with uncanny accuracy the long course of the war. Both North and South, their reason blinded by the moment's passion, expected a quick and easy triumph, but Sam reported that "more rational people" in the South foresaw the North getting whipped in the early battles because its troops would be poorly trained and led, but feared that northern resources would be too much for them in the long haul. Nevertheless, he reported, southerners were grimly determined to fight to the bitter end, even if it meant martyrdom.

As Russell and Sam continued their tour into the deep South, Sam described for Seward the defenses of Savannah and Mobile. In New Orleans he found only a small detachment of artillery about to leave for Richmond with "*no horses.*" Summing up his impression after he and Russell had reached Cairo, Illinois, Sam wrote Seward:

"For your purpose, you will need 500,000 men and a million in all before the end of the year. This, with half a million reserves, will give you a butcher's axe to draw upon when you fight an engagement. It must be a bloody riot that lands you in Richmond."

No prediction could have been less welcome. The fevered North was swept by the battle cry "On to Richmond!" as if all the Union troops had to do was to parade south to an easy victory. Such public pressure forced the premature thrust into Virginia that led to crushing and humiliating defeat in the First Battle of Bull Run. It was a Union bloodbath that demonstrated just how right Sam Ward had been, but being right did Sam little good.

He was now in a financial bind, not an unusual circumstance with him, and he had been hoping for a diplomatic appointment from Seward to rescue his sagging fortunes the way the earlier Paraguayan mission had. But the secretary, though he accepted gladly all the information Sam furnished, balked at passing out rewards.

Back in Washington, hopping back and forth between the capital and New York on mysterious missions, Sam Ward, the suave cosmopolitan with contacts everywhere, picked up and forwarded to Seward the first tip about French plans to establish a puppet emperor in Mexico. Taking advantage of the North's absorption in fratricidal war, France and Spain, with the connivance of Britain, decided this was their chance to reestablish an important colony in the New World. Sam had had connections in México City ever since his first lobbying mission there in the days of Santa Anna. On November 6, 1861, he wrote Seward that a completely reliable source had informed him Emperor Napoleon III of France was plotting an invasion of Mexico.

He wrote that "it has been settled in Paris and Madrid, and not discountenanced in London, that the 'Mexicans shall have a throne—republics have proved all folly and failure.' "

Sam's information was accurate, as usual. Just four months later, a joint French-Spanish-British expedition seized the custom house at Vera Cruz on the pretext of compelling the payment of Mexico's foreign debts.

Denied public employment, Sam struggled along through the war years, turning a fast dollar wherever possible and devoting himself in his idle hours to an old love, poetry. He worked long enough and hard enough to produce a volume of poems, published in 1865, but, though some critics were kind, it soon became apparent even to Sam that he would never be another Longfellow.

Following the assassination of Lincoln and the installation of Vice-president Andrew Johnson in the White House, Sam's fortunes took a dramatic turn for the better. One of Sam's friends—the man always had friends everywhere—was Hugh McCulloch, the secretary of the treasury. McCulloch sought to reestablish order in the nation's finances by retiring some $450 million in greenbacks issued during the feverish wartime spending, but he was fearful that dimwitted congressmen, not understanding the complexities of the issue, would vote down the proposal. Needing an ambassador of goodwill, he turned to Sam Ward.

Sam's method of persuasion was the one he always used when he had sufficient finances. Long experience had taught him that the fastest route to mental conversion lay through a well-satisfied stomach. So now, with the government's financing, he set about the gratifying task of pampering some of the most impressive paunches in Washington.

He rented a shabby little house at 1406 E Street and began to serve the most elegant dinners capital society had ever known. As one historian later recalled: "He made dining an art, did his own marketing, bought his own wines, imported his own coffee and tea from Brazil and China." Sam's niece, Maud Howe Elliott, later described an elaborate dinner he gave in Sutherland's Restaurant on Liberty Street in downtown New York.

"The pièce de résistance," she wrote, "was a dish of beavers' tails—a dainty famous in the old Hudson's Bay Company's feasts. The large, flat tails were sauté with a wonderful Béchamel sauce. I wrote an article for *Harper's Bazar,* describing this delicacy, that attracted more attention than anything I ever wrote. I received letters from all over the world asking: 'Is this true?' 'Can that be so?' "

With beaver tails and other exotic fare making him the talk of New York and Washington, Sam Ward now began his long reign as King of the Lobby, a period of power that covered the years 1865–80. He had a hand in everything: in the affairs of transcontinental railroads, telegraph companies, lotteries, in an abortive plan to annex the Caribbean island of Santo Domingo, and in Brazilian railways.

Usually all his dinner guests were male, and the rule at his gatherings was absolute discretion. As a result, politicians who might be bitterly opposed to each other were able to meet under Sam's benign influence, engage in the best conversation in Washington, achieve a rosy glow from his vintage wines (he never served hard liquor)—and know that whatever they said would go no further. Sam never offered a bribe or used the threat of blackmail. He simply relied on the camaraderie cultivated at the table to do its work for him. When a measure in which he was especially interested was coming up for a vote in the House or Senate, one of his erstwhile guests who might need a little urging in the right direction would receive a simple note on tinted blue paper, reading: "This is my little lamb. Be good. Sam Ward!"

By such measures, Sam helped Treasury Secretary McCulloch get some of the financial reforms he wanted through Congress, and McCulloch's recommendation brought him other clients. One was John

Morrissey, a stalwart in New York's Tammany Hall Democratic organization and a former prizefighter known as "Old Smoke." Morrissey ran
the largest gambling and lottery operation in New York, and he conceived a novel idea: he wanted his business taxed. A man asking to have
his business taxed is as rare as a man biting a dog, but Morrissey was not
crazy. He was, on the contrary, fox-clever. He reasoned that his operation was so huge and remunerative that he could afford to pay a tax, but
many of his less affluent rivals could not. A tax would drive them out of
business—and give Morrissey more business. Sam Ward, ever ready to
oblige for a fee, got the tax measure Morrissey wanted through Congress, and the word spread that Sam was the man to see to "get things
done" in Washington.

Services like these often earned Sam fees running well into five
figures; but, however much he earned, he always managed to spend it
almost before he got it. He might start out in the morning with a
thousand dollars in his pocket, and by nightfall he would have given
away or loaned every last dollar of it and be without the money to pay
cab fare home.

★

One of Sam's favorite hangouts in Washington, when he was not
entertaining in his own home, was Welcher's Restaurant, which probably served the best food in the capital. Sam became such a fixture there
that many got the impression he was the proprietor. Actually, he had no
financial interest in the restaurant, but he mingled there with all manner of politicians for whom it was a popular rendezvous. From some of
these contacts he picked up the first hint of a major political upheaval,
the attempt of Republican Radicals in Congress to impeach President
Johnson.

Johnson had attempted to follow Lincoln's policy of moderation
toward the defeated South, but the Radicals in Congress wanted ven-
geance. In February, 1868, they decided to impeach Johnson, oust him
from office, and set up what would be virtually a congressional committee dictatorship. Sam Ward, in addition to being sympathetic to
Johnson's humane policies, was opposed in principle to this effort to
scrap the Constitution.

It was at Welcher's on February 22, Washington's birthday, that
Sam learned the details and timetable of the Republican Radical plot.
He hurried at once to Secretary McCulloch.

"I took a card from him to the President, whom I did not know," Sam later wrote. "He was entertaining the diplomatic corps at dinner, and I had an hour to spare which I consumed in seeing Chief Justice [Salmon P.] Chase, to whom the news was a surprise. It was also news to the President, when I found him at ten o'clock, and told him to secure the ablest counsel, half Democrats and half Republicans."

This advice was followed, one of Johnson's Republican defense attorneys being William M. Evarts, a close friend of Sam's. As Sam had warned, the Radicals lost no time. The House voted impeachment, and Johnson was rushed to trial before the Senate on March 5.

The evidence indicates that Sam played a busy, behind-the-scenes role in the struggle that followed. Though the charges against Johnson had been trumped up and had no validity, Sam at first expected the President to be convicted. But as time went on and he worked his wiles, he became more optimistic. He exerted all his arts of persuasion, helped to raise defense funds, contributed heavily from his own pocket, and brought important politicians and influential personages together in the adroit lobbying manner he knew so well. By the time the vote was taken on May 16, Sam was confident enough to wire his cousin, Charles H. Ward, the Wall Street broker: "The last vote on the list has the cast. He was safe last night." And safe he remained. When Senator Edmund G. Ross voted "not guilty," President Johnson was acquitted by a single vote.

Throughout the rest of his life, Sam Ward looked back on the subtle role he had played during the impeachment crisis as his proudest accomplishment. Years afterward, he wrote: "I am prouder to have countermined that vile intrigue . . . than of any other event in my life. I contributed my money and efforts and we won, and I saved the country from being Mexicanized."

A man who wielded such influence that he helped to save a president had all kinds of clients pleading for his help for all kinds of reasons. In one letter to Longfellow, Sam explained that one client, whose favorite measure was apparently in jeopardy in a committee, was anxious to see that a hostile committeeman did not arrive to cast his vote before noon, when the committee was to adjourn. The client offered Sam $5,000 if he could delay the arrival of the hostile legislator. Sam, obviously chuckling to himself as he wrote, told Longfellow that he had achieved this desired end "by having his boots mislaid, while I smoked a cigar and condoled with him until they could be found at

11:45! I had the satisfaction of a good laugh, a good fee in my pocket, and of having prevented a conspiracy!"

Sam was now a man of such large affairs that his interests at times sent him off roaming the world. In midwinter, 1871, he once more whirled around Europe, seeking out Emperor Dom Pedro II of Brazil. The emperor was staying in Florence, Italy, and Sam, representing British railway interests, had a proposition to discuss with him.

The emperor at first was unapproachable. He was traveling incognito and sent emphatic word that he would *not* see Sam Ward. Even an emperor could not make such a rejection stick when Sam had set his mind on persuasion. Knowing Dom Pedro was an ardent bookman, Sam had brought along an autographed copy of Longfellow's latest volume of poetry. He sent this to the emperor with a courteous note, and the effect was almost magical. The royal whim did a somersault—Sam was welcomed heartily, and he and Dom Pedro conversed for an hour. The emperor expressed a desire to meet Longfellow, and Sam, as one of the poet's oldest and closest friends, assured him this would be the easiest thing in the world to arrange. After that, Sam got around to his real purpose—railroad projects in Brazil—and he and Dom Pedro parted the best of friends.

Back in Washington, lobbying and corruption had become such a scandal that the House Ways and Means Committee finally launched an investigation. The *New York Tribune* charged in 1875 that $1 million had been used to corrupt Congress and secure a fat subsidy for the Pacific Mail Steamship Company to carry mail to China and the Orient. The subsidy had been justified publicly on the grounds it would make possible the building of American ships to carry the mails, ending the reliance on foreign-flag vessels.

To the astonishment of his friends, Sam Ward was subpoenaed to testify before the committee. A payoff agent had produced a list of persons who had shared in one kitty of $120,000. Named were newspaper editors; Washington correspondents; ex-postmasters; a former mayor of Washington, James G. Barrett—and Sam Ward. Barrett and Ward were said to have split $7,000. Sam promptly acknowledged that he had received $4,000. He had spent it in Welcher's long since, he said, and he went blithely off to testify before the committee.

He told the investigators he had considered the subsidy bill "a good measure" because "our shipbuilding was going to the dogs" and some stimulus was needed to keep the American flag flying on the seas.

He would have helped the Pacific Mail Steamship Company "without one cent of compensation," he said, but when Barrett came to him and proposed a fee, who was he to turn it down? Actually, he said, he had had to do very little for the money since there was so much sentiment in Congress in favor of the bill, and he really didn't know why anyone would have hired him unless it was that they wanted the prestige of "the King."

Sam insisted he hadn't known about payouts to anyone else until he read the list of names in the newspapers. Asked if he had ever heard of bribes being paid in connection with the legislation, Sam was positive. Not a penny had been paid as far as he knew, he said.

This much established, Sam Ward launched into a lecture on the perils and rewards of lobbying. He was his usual witty, urbane self, and he soon had members of the investigating committee convulsed with laughter.

"This business of lobbying, so called, is as precarious as fishing in the Hebrides," he said. "You get all ready, your boats go out—suddenly there comes a storm, and away you are driven." Ten measures, sometimes fifty, fail for one that is carried, he explained, "but once in a while a pleasant little windfall like this recompenses us . . ." Then he described a lobbyist's life in these words:

"To introduce a bill properly, to have it referred to the proper committee, to see that some member on that committee understands its merits, to attend to it, to watch it, to have a counsel go and advocate it before the committee, to see that members of the committee do not oversleep on the mornings of important meetings, to watch for the coming of the bill to Congress day after day, week after week, to have your men on hand a dozen times, and to have them as often disappointed; to have one of those storms which spring up in the Adriatic of Congress, until your men are worried, and worn, and tired, and until they say to themselves that they will not go up to the Capitol today, —and then to have the bird suddenly flushed, and all your preparations brought to naught,—these are some of the experiences of the lobby."

Sam's audience was laughing heartily by this time, and its members continued to be amused, their probe virtually forgotten, as Sam explained his good-host technique. "There is nothing in the world so excellent as entertainments of a refined order," he told the committee. One dour member asked him: "Is there not a great deal of money wasted on good dinners?"

The question, to Sam, was heresy, and swift as lightning came his reply: "I do not think money is ever wasted on a good dinner. If a man dines badly, he forgets to say his prayers before going to bed, but if he dines well he feels like a saint."

He left them laughing, stepping down from the witness chair with the triumphant air of a marshal of the armies of France.

It was a colorful, climactic moment in the life of a unique man. Sam Ward lived a life that was full of surprises and amazing turns of fortune, and nothing in it was more surprising, more amazing, than the fairy-tale episode that brightened his last years.

The roots went back to the 1850s, when Sam was in California. He had found a young man, James Robert Keene, alone, friendless—and desperately ill. With the kindliness that was natural to him, Sam stayed with Keene and nursed him back to health. He took no particular credit for the deed (he performed many similar compassionate acts during his life), but Keene never forgot. After Sam left California, Keene became the most successful stock plunger in San Francisco. He amassed $4 million and became president of the San Francisco Stock Exchange.

In 1877 Keene and his wife decided to take a vacation and visit Europe. Arriving in New York, Keene looked up Sam Ward. Curious about Wall Street, Keene expressed a desire to meet some of the more notable stock manipulators, and Sam, who knew everybody, introduced him to Jay Gould and others. Keene soon became so intrigued by the greater possibilities of the Wall Street market that he called off his trip to Europe, and within a year, by daring raids on various stocks, he had built his $4 million into $13 million. In the process, he decided to take Sam Ward along with him on the merry ride to fortune. Keene was manipulating railroad stocks at the time, and he bought a large bloc in Sam's name, held the stocks until he had driven the market up—then sold out and deposited nearly $1 million to Sam's credit in the bank of J. P. Morgan and Company.

One million dollars in the days of nickel beer should have been enough to let Sam live like a nabob for the rest of his life, but Sam Ward, though he had once been a banker, was one of those men who should never have been entrusted with more than a fixed weekly allowance. He began to spend with a lavish hand, and though some of his spending did credit to the generous impulses of his heart, much of it did discredit to his head.

Julia Ward Howe's husband had died, leaving her all but impoverished, so Sam surprised her by buying her a fine house on Beacon

Street in Boston and sending lamps, rugs, curtains, and other furnishings to make her comfortable. Another sister, Louisa Crawford, who had married the artist Luther Terry after the death of Thomas Crawford, was living in Italy, where she, too, had fallen on hard times, having lost most of her fortune in the panic of 1873. Sam showered her with checks, arranged a vacation for her and her family in Switzerland, and in 1881 brought Louisa and her daughter, Daisy Terry, to America for a family reunion.

Sam had so much money now that he could afford such family beneficences, but unfortunately he could not limit himself to them. The truth was that Sam was an easy mark, a sucker, and it was not long before two fast-talking promoters managed to separate him from the bulk of his fortune. They talked him into bankrolling a scheme to make Long Beach, Long Island, outshine the fanciest seashore resort of the day, Long Branch, New Jersey. These scoundrels swindled some $500,000 from Sam and persuaded him, in addition, to sign notes making himself responsible for heavy borrowings incurred in the Long Beach promotion.

By 1882 Sam's final fortune had almost melted away, and he wrote Julia: "I have never been so wretched as since I got some money." Despite his worries, he was still the impeccable host, the boon companion—and he was still astute enough and wily enough to launch another notable career.

Louisa's son, F. Marion Crawford, was a young man in the throes of indecision about his future role in life. He had gone to India, where he had edited a newspaper. Then he came to New York, where, fortunately, he fell under the benign patronage of Uncle Sam. Encouraged and guided by Sam, young Crawford wrote several articles on social and economic issues for the more intellectual periodicals of the day, but such writing did not seem to offer much opportunity for the future.

Crawford, however, had a fund of stories about India, and one, about a diamond merchant whom he had met, fascinated Sam. Among Sam's many acquaintances was a young, ambitious salesman in Macmillan's New York book store—George Brett. Sam casually suggested that Brett have dinner with him and his nephew. During the meal, Sam steered the conversation to Crawford's adventures in India and got his nephew to tell the story of the diamond merchant. Crawford told it so well that, when he finished, Brett thumped the table and said, "There is no question what you should do, Mr. Crawford—write out that story!" And Sam added, "Write it now!"

Crawford took the advice. He returned to Uncle Sam's apartment and began to write. Weeks later, at his Aunt Julia's farm, Oak Glen, he finished the manuscript of his first novel, *Mr. Isaacs*. The book was an immediate best seller in both the United States and England, and F. Marion Crawford was launched on a career that would make him one of the most popular novelists of the 1890–early 1900s period.

Sam's own circumstances were now desperate. To avoid subpoenas in connection with the Long Beach debts, he sailed surreptitiously for England. There he was hailed with great warmth by a host of friends and was lionized by English society. Every day was a party, and peers of the realm vied for his sparkling company.

From England, he went on to Italy to join Louisa and her family. In Naples he was felled by a raging fever, apparently caused by ptomaine from eating tainted seafood. He dragged himself back to Louisa in Rome, so ill it was feared he would die. He rallied, however. He appeared to recover and went to the seacoast town of Pegli some six miles from Genoa. F. Marion Crawford, Daisy Terry, and a nurse stayed with him. He dictated letters to friends all over the world, seemingly with all his old verve and wit. But then suddenly, on May 19, 1884, his system collapsed and he drifted off peacefully into his final sleep. He was buried in a little Protestant cemetery on the crest of a hill shaded by ilex trees and oaks, thousands of miles from those power centers of New York and Washington where he had ruled as the King of the Lobby.

The longest lobbying campaign in American history—and the one that had the most far-reaching effects on the whole society—was the so-called temperance movement, which for much of its life was anything but temperate. It was a campaign that lasted one hundred and twelve years before it finally resulted in the 1920 Prohibition Amendment banning the sale of all liquor.

The long, persistent, and often violent drive to turn Americans into a nation of teetotalers had its wellsprings in the excesses of a hard-drinking past. Though it is fashionable to gild our colonial and Revolutionary ancestors with the halos of saints, the undeniable fact is that they swilled an astonishing amount of heady brews. It was customary to begin the day at breakfast with a tankard of ale, or something even stronger, and the day progressed with a steady stream of libations that left many in a stupor by nightfall.

The Reverend Mason L. ("Parson") Weems, the biographer who propagated many of the early myths about George Washington, wrote a pamphlet called "The Drunkard's Looking Glass." In this he reproduced verbatim a tavern bill run up on April 1, 1812, by a Mr. Thomas C——. This showed that Mr. C fortified himself for the rigors of the day in this fashion: three mint slings before breakfast, nine tumblers of grog before dinner, three glasses of wine and bitters, two ticklers of French brandy, and wine with his supper.

No class of society was immune from the imbibing custom of the times, not even the clergy. The Reverend Leonard Woods, veteran professor at Andover

5

TEMPERANCE?

Theological Seminary, could "reckon up among my acquaintances forty ministers who were either drunkards, or so far addicted to drinking that their reputation and usefulness were greatly impaired, if not utterly ruined." His was not the only reference to pastors weaving their way to their pulpits on unsteady feet. In Albany, according to an elder of the cloth, more than half the clergy drank heavily, and some were completely besotted.

Several of the outstanding leaders of the Revolutionary War period were alarmed by the drunken excesses of the age, but even they could do little about it. Benjamin Franklin was foreman of a grand jury that denounced the universal swilling and expressed the opinion that poverty and other evils were being fostered by the taverns and tippling houses with which Philadelphia abounded. In Boston, John Adams, who was to become the nation's second President, applied to the Court of Sessions to reduce the number of licensed dispensaries, which, he said, spawned "idlers, thieves, sots and consumptive patients." He was denounced as a "hypocrite and ambitious demagog" for his pains. In later life he abandoned hope of curbing his fellowmen's addiction to rum, and, in doing so, he fired a parting blast, declaring that it was in the taverns where "diseases, vicious habits, bastards and legislators are frequently begotten."

Since excess is the father of counter-excess, there is little wonder that in a society literally awash in grog there should then emerge a fanatical movement to ban all spiritous liquors under the false banner of total abstinence, labeled "temperance."

To fix a precise day and time when it all began, one has to go to the evening of April 30, 1808. Dr. Billy J. Clark, a young doctor in the hamlet of Moreau in New York's upstate Saratoga County, was sitting before the fireplace in his home, reading a pamphlet. The text that had fallen into his hands was entitled "An Inquiry into the Effect of Spiritous Liquors on the Human Body and Mind," and it had been written in 1785 by none other than Dr. Benjamin Rush, of Philadelphia, a signer of the Declaration of Independence, the surgeon general of the Continental Army, and the foremost medical authority of his day.

Dr. Rush described graphically the evil effects of hard liquor as he had observed them in camp and town (he was not, it must be stressed, opposed to wines and beer, which he considered beneficial), and he summed up his conclusions in this description of the victim of firewater:

"Ardent spirits causes him in folly to resemble a calf; in stupidity, an ass; in roaring, a mad bull; in quarreling and fighting, a dog; in cruelty, a tiger; in fetor, a skunk; in filthiness, a hog; and in obscenity, a he-goat."

Dr. Clark, who had treated hard-drinking lumberjacks whom he had found in delirium tremens, recognized all the elements of that description. Fired by a sudden zeal, he leaped to horse like Paul Revere and rode off into the night to the home of his friend, the Reverend Lebbeus Armstrong, pastor of Moreau's First Congregational Church. "We must do something!" he cried in effect—and with that cry, the "temperance movement" was born.

Throughout the next century, the campaign to curb the drunken habits of Americans was to have its ups and downs, at times raging full force like a stormy sea, at others subsiding into defeated placidity—only to rise again, more intemperate, more determined, more passionate than ever. Among the many thousands who participated in the fanatical effort that was to saddle the nation with Prohibition, two names stand out: those of an Amazon named Carry A. Nation, who went around smashing up barrooms with her hatchet, and of Wayne Bidwell Wheeler, the ruthless and astute lobbyist who masterminded the final pressure campaign to ruin the political careers of any politicians who sided with the liquor interests.

Mrs. Nation and her hatchet came upon the scene as the result of an aroused women's movement. The Civil War had been a boon to carousing, as wars always are, and many states that had been pressured into passing prohibition laws repealed them. "Temperance" was at a low ebb when the so-called Women's Crusade began to march through Ohio, leading to the birth of the Women's Christian Temperance Union. The WCTU, as it was to be popularly known, was founded at a meeting in the Second Presbyterian Church in Cleveland in 1874, and it attracted to its ranks a remarkable woman, Frances Willard.

Miss Willard had been a schoolteacher, but once she enlisted in the cause, she proved to be an inspiring leader, and within five years she was president of the WCTU. She raised money, made converts, and established local WCTU branches in almost every city, town, and hamlet in the nation. Among her many notable victories was the conversion of the White House during the presidency of Rutherford B. Hayes. Mrs. Hayes and Miss Willard were friends, and the President's wife announced that, not only would liquor not be served at public functions in the White House, it wouldn't be served privately at the President's own table.

On a broader front, WCTU pressure compelled virtually every state legislature to order the compulsory teaching of the dangers of alcohol in the public schools. And some states even began to enact dry laws. One of these was Kansas, and the Kansas statute set the stage for the emergence on the national scene of the incredible Carry Nation.

Born Carry Amelia Moore—her first name spelled oddly because her father was a man of imperfect learning—she grew into a woman five feet, eleven and a half inches tall, weighing a hard-muscled 175 pounds. Her heritage was not notable for mental balance. Her mother lived for years under the delusion that she was Queen Victoria, finally dying in the Missouri State Hospital for the Insane. Carry's delusion took more practical form. According to her, the Lord talked personally to her and instructed her to go out and smash up saloons.

Carry had reason to abhor liquor in all its forms. Her first husband, Dr. Charles Gloyd, had gone to the altar on their wedding day reeking of alcohol, and within six months he had been deposited in a drunkard's grave. Carry waited ten years before committing herself again to matrimony, and her choice the second time did little more credit to her discernment. Husband number two was David Nation, an incompetent who called himself an editor and posed sometimes as a lawyer, at others as a minister of the Gospel.

Nation was enough of a trial as a husband to set any woman to brooding, and Carry, while her husband was in one of his preaching phases in Medicine Lodge, Kansas, began brooding to serious purpose during her tête-à-têtes with the Lord. Kansas was technically dry as the result of the liquor ban Frances Willard had fostered, but in reality it was just as wet as the entire nation was to become during the later, technically dry era of Prohibition.

Carry Nation, who had been elected president of the Barber County chapter of the WCTU, found this state of affairs intolerable, and she wrote appeals to the governor, the attorney general, the sheriff, and various newspapers, clamoring for someone to close "the joints." None of the officials bothered even to answer her. That was a mistake. Carry Nation was not a woman to be ignored.

On the afternoon of June 5, 1900, according to her own account, she squeezed her eyes tight shut, took a pin, and jabbed it at random into her open Bible. When she opened her eyes, she found the pin standing like a battle standard in these lines in the sixtieth chapter of Isaiah: "Arise, shine; for thy light is come, and the glory of the Lord is risen upon thee."

The message, it might seem to the skeptical, was a little vague, lacking in essential details. Arise—how? Shine—where? Carry was not left long in doubt, for naturally, divine guidance would not leave matters in such an uncertain state. It was only a few minutes, she always averred, before a musical voice murmured a command that made all clear:

"Go to Kiowa! Take something in your hands and throw at those places and smash them!"

Kiowa was known as "the wettest town in Barber County," and so it was the logical target for minions of the Lord. Carry rose the next morning, filled with holy zeal. She collected an arsenal of bricks, which she wrapped in old newspapers. Then she hitched up the Nations' horse, Old Prince, and drove in the family buggy twenty miles to Kiowa.

One of the more prominent joints in town was known as Dobson's, run by a man whose brother happened to be the county sheriff. Arriving at Dobson's, Mrs. Nation hitched Old Prince to the hitching post, loaded her arms with all the missiles she could carry, and pushed open the door of the saloon.

Dobson was behind the bar, polishing glasses and whistling a happy, proprietorial tune. Half a dozen men, with heads that seemed to want to split apart, had bellied up to the bar for the morning pickup. They had not yet succeeded in this laudable endeavor when a booming voice seemed to shatter their aching craniums.

"Men! I have come to save you from a drunkard's grave!" Carry shouted.

Red-rimmed eyes turned to stare at the tall, sturdy figure, dressed in a hideous black alpaca dress, bonnet on her head. And at that moment, the first brick sailed through the air, smashing into the elegant, gilt-framed mirror behind the bar and sending slivers of glass flying.

"Now, Mother Nation—" Dobson began. He got no further. Carry had an arm that would have done credit to a major-league pitcher, and she hurled her second bolt with unerring accuracy.

It wiped out every glass on the back bar and smashed several bottles. After that, the rain of missiles came so fast that Dobson and his shocked clientele scuttled into remote corners of the dive, seeking safety. Horror-struck, almost moaning in their anguish, they watched their favorite beverages destroyed before their eyes while Mrs. Nation accompanied her uncannily accurate pitching with a hymn: "Who Hath Sorrow? Who Hath Woe?"

Dobson and his customers might have told her, but Carry was not in a listening mood. She had finished her wrecking chore and turned to leave the bar when her eyes lighted on a rocking chair. There, she later insisted, she saw the seated image of President William McKinley, gently rocking back and forth and mocking her efforts.

With a shriek of rage, Carry grabbed the last of her bricks, and with one final, herculean throw, she reduced the chair to splinters and wiped out the presidential sneer.

"Now, Mr. Dobson," Carry cried, "I have finished. God be with you."

Dobson, crouched in his corner, was almost in a state of cardiac arrest, and neither his mental nor physical condition was improved when Carry reached the street. For there she noticed that she had not quite finished her task: Dobson's plate-glass windows in the front of his saloon were still whole. It was an oversight quickly remedied. Seizing two more bricks from the floor of her buggy, Carry hurled them through the windows and, to the sound of shattering glass, drove off down the street.

A block away, there was another pub with an early-morning clientele seeking relief from the horrors of the night before. Proprietor and customers were all too preoccupied with this most worthy task to notice the black-clad apparition that walked in, brick-laden. Their first warning of disaster came with the fusillade that smashed the bar mirror, shattered glasses, and destroyed bottles. In little more than seconds, the proprietor later vowed, his haven of solace was reduced to a shambles, and his first thought was that the devil himself must be paying him a visit. But Mrs. Nation quickly disabused him about the source of trouble, calling, as she left, her favorite "God be with you!"

Carry had one stop left on her Kiowa itinerary, the Lewis Bar. She descended on this as she had on the others, but she was now encountering a difficulty—lack of ammunition. She ran out of bricks before she had wrecked more than two thirds of the place. Balked, furious, she looked around for something else to throw, and there in the recreation area she spotted billiard balls. Grabbing up these substitute missiles, she resumed her cannonading with even greater vigor.

Several prints of sporting figures and of actresses not too fully clad adorned the walls, and these, with cries of outrage, she ripped down and tore to pieces. She overturned tables, kicked the rungs out of chairs, drop-kicked a cuspidor over the black iron stove, smashed out the front windows—and then, in a final fury, turned her attention to the one object that had defied her. It was the long, ornamental mirror behind the bar, and it was made of such heavy glass that one of her bricks had bounced off it. Not only that, Mrs. Nation later vowed, but right where her brick had struck so futilely, the face of Satan had appeared, grinning and sticking out his tongue at her, waggling his horns, and in general making an ass of himself. Shrieking with outrage at this defiance, Mrs. Nation wound up her pitching arm and hurled a billiard ball with such force that it made a spherical hole in the mirror and buried itself in the wall directly behind the spot where the devil had so incautiously leered at her.

Thankful that she had given the monster a headache if not, indeed, a hole in the head, Mrs. Nation cried out, "Thanks, God!" And on this note she departed.

By this time several hundred persons had gathered, pushing and shoving in the narrow street to see what was happening. They fell back before the Amazonian figure that strode from the bar, bonnet askew upon her head, her black alpaca rumpled, wet, and reeking with the hated fumes of alcohol, her hands dirty, and her ample bosom panting and heaving from her exertions. Noticing their stares, Carry whirled on the crowd, crying, "Men of Kiowa, I have destroyed three of your places of business! If I have broken a statute of the state of Kansas, put me in jail. If I am not a lawbreaker, your Mayor and Councilmen are. You must arrest one of us."

The town marshal stepped forward, taking Old Prince's reins and leading him and his mistress down the street to the spot where the mayor and one of the irate saloonkeepers were trying to decide what to do. The proprietor wanted compensation for his wrecked establishment, but Mrs. Nation, drawing herself up to her full height in the wagon, glared down at the mayor and told him, "I won't do it. You are a partner of the dive keeper and the statutes hold you responsible. . . . Now if you won't arrest me, I'll go home."

There followed a comic-opera scene. The mayor, Mrs. Nation, and the saloonkeeper were gathered around her wagon. Some fifty yards down the street huddled the city attorney and city councilmen. The attorney scurried back and forth between the two groups like a worried hen with feathers aflutter while the town dignitaries tried to decide what to do about Carry—and while their watching constituents began to show signs of relishing their predicament.

It was probably the most ridiculous impromptu meeting of a town governing body ever held. The nub of the problem, of course, was that Mrs. Nation undeniably had destroyed a lot of property—but, as the city attorney finally said, "it was property being put to an illegal use," a concession that the WCTU seized upon with howls of glee. All the time, as official minds teetered back and forth in indecision, Mrs. Nation stood erect in her wagon, bellowing at the top of her lungs her favorite hymn: "Who Hath Sorrow? Who Hath Woe?"

Everybody, it became clear, had sorrow and woe except Carry Nation, the one-woman task force that had caused all the trouble. The town fathers, finally conceding that they couldn't use the law against this Amazonian law-enforcer, decided to do nothing. At a word from the mayor, the marshal dropped Old Prince's reins in disgust and told Mrs. Nation, "Go home."

The Kiowa raid was a mere zephyr compared to the hurricane to come. Carry's violent brand of campaigning shocked the head of the state WCTU, a lady who announced that the organization "could not accept responsibility for the smashing at Kiowa." Carry retorted that the lady's husband had just been given a job as resident physician of the state reformatory, "a transparent bribe." Having triumphed in that exchange, Carry prepared for her next grand assault—this time on the notoriously wet city of Wichita with its forty-odd joints called "sample rooms."

Carry knew she would have to travel by train, and so she could hardly lug an arsenal of bricks with her. New weapons were required, and she found them handy in her home. One was Nation's stout walking cane; another, an iron rod a foot long "and as large around as my thumb." She put the iron rod in a valise along with some toilet articles and a Bible, and on December 26, 1900, she boarded a train for Wichita.

She wore the battle garb that was soon to make her a favorite with the nation's cartoonists: the black alpaca dress with big black pearl buttons up one side, a white bow around her throat, a dark poke bonnet tied by a silk ribbon under her chin, multiple petticoats, black cotton stockings, heavy, square-toed shoes, and a warm cape of navy-blue cloth.

Carry reached Wichita at 7 P.M. and registered in a dingy hotel near the railroad station. Then she set out to see what there was to see—and what she saw was something she could never have imagined.

Her researches took her eventually to the basement bar of the Hotel Carey, an elegant sample room that had been praised from coast to coast. The bar itself was a magnificent sight, more than fifty feet long, curved and made of solid cherry that was polished to a high sheen to reflect the glare of a hundred lights. The brilliance was enough to blind one, coming in out of the night. But it was not the bar itself that bedazzled Carry. Behind it stretched an enormous oil painting, *Cleopatra at the Bath*.

The Egyptian temptress was sprawled seductively upon a couch, quite nude, with a neat little patch of pubic hair showing. Her Roman and Egyptian handmaidens, who were presumably preparing the bath, were likewise revealed in full anatomical detail, and two huge eunuchs, busily fanning flies away, wore only breechclouts. Carry looked at this tableau, gasped, and came to a shocked standstill.

She was speechless—but only for a moment. Fury replaced shock. According to eyewitnesses later, she emitted what some described as a "screek," others as a "shrill, thin 'Yawk!' " Then she marched up to the bar, where an innocent-looking young man was polishing glasses.

"Young man, what are you doing here?" Carry demanded, a foolish question in view of the obvious—but then the sight of Cleopatra had addled Carry.

The young bartender looked up, misunderstood the import of the question, and said, "I'm sorry, madam, we don't serve ladies."

"*Serve me!*" Carry screeched. "Do you think I'd drink the hellish poison you've got here? What is that naked woman doing up there?"

Still calm, the young bartender told her, "That's only a picture, madam."

"It's disgraceful!" Carry shrieked. "You're insulting your mother by having her form stripped naked and hung up in a place where it is not even decent for a woman to be when she has her clothes on!"

Baffled at this linking of his mother with Cleopatra at her ablutions, the young bartender bowed courteously to Carry, then retreated to the end of the bar, surrendering the field. Several men, "sampling" at the tables, had witnessed the encounter, and one rose, offering to buy Carry a drink.

At the suggestion, she yowled with rage like a banshee, and, beside herself, she grabbed a bottle from the bar, smashed it to smithereens upon the floor—and then fled out into the night.

Back in her hotel room, she tied the iron bar to the end of the heavy cane with stout cord, and from the street she selected "some of the nicest rocks, round with sharp edges." These she apparently stored in capacious pockets in her cape. The cane-cudgel could be easily hidden under that garment's flowing folds. So armed, she set out the next morning for the Hotel Carey.

Bartender Edward Parker was dispensing medication to seven clients in desperate need. Without warning, a hard-thrown rock whizzed overhead, smashing the painting's glass screen and ripping through the canvas some three inches from Cleopatra's left knee.

The first projectile was followed by a second, and finally a third shot shattered the elegant Venetian mirror behind the bar. "Cost fifteen hunnert dollars," bartender Parker moaned to police afterward.

With the mirror reduced to glass shards, Carry emitted her first battle cry: "Glory to God! Peace on earth, good will to men!"

Far from reassured by this pious utterance, bartender and clientele fled like badgers burrowing for safety. Carry, all potential opposition routed, whipped out her iron-tipped cane and rushed up and down the bar, flailing away at everything in sight.

Pandemonium swept through the hotel. Guests raised windows and yelled at the top of their lungs, "Help! Help! Police!"

Detective Park Massey, responding to the emergency, entered the bar to find himself wading through a sea of glass and spilled liquor —and to find Carry Nation beating "a great brass spittoon," the only object left to whack, into a shapeless lump of metal.

"Madam, I must place you under arrest," Massey said.

"Arrest *me!*" Carry howled. "Why don't you arrest the man who runs this hell-hole? Don't you know this is against the law? Can't you smell the rotten poison?"

She invited Massey to sniff, but the detective, who had no need to sniff, insisted firmly, "You are destroying property, madam. I must arrest you."

Just as in Kiowa, Carry represented a delicate judicial problem. How could the authorities prosecute her when, in essence, she had been doing the kind of raiding a vigilant law-enforcement agency should have done? It was all most embarrassing for the official establishment of Wichita, and Carry was finally released on the specious pretext that a considerate prosecutor feared for her mental condition.

There was, of course, nothing wrong with Carry's mental condition—at least, it was no different from what it had ever been. But there was one change: Carry had attracted national attention. She became within a few months a whirling, avenging dervish. During 1901 she conducted more than a score of raids, leaving havoc and official consternation in her wake, but one foray stood out above all others—the attack on Topeka that put Carry and her hatchet into cartoons across the nation.

This sharp-edged weapon, which was to become the symbol of Carry, the saloon smasher, had come into her hand quite by accident. She had returned on January 21, 1901, to Wichita, where she had aroused her followers to fever pitch with her passionate, revivalist oratory against the demon rum. Some of her frenzied fans informed her that one of them had a cellar in which there was a delightful assortment of "iron bars, chunks of scrap metal and stones." And there Carry found her first hatchet. Whirling it about her head as a Crusader might have twirled his battle-ax, Carry led her women's army against the Douglas Avenue sample room of James Burns, where she wreaked total destruction. The experience convinced her that a hatchet, with its sharp cutting edge, was a much more effective weapon than a brick.

As a result, five days after this discovery, Carry went to Topeka to "free the Capital of Kansas from the shame of its saloons." She was well known as a one-woman menace by this time, and her arrival precipitated a small riot in which she was roughly handled by devotees of intemperance. Undeterred, Carry bought four well-honed hatchets for eighty-five cents apiece, and with these she armed herself and two followers.

To take the foe by surprise, the little band set out at the unlikely hour of 6 A.M., as a heavy snow was falling. Carry led her followers to the Senate Bar, Topeka's most elite establishment, the favorite watering spa for city officials, state legislators, and judges. The bartender, Benner Tucker, had no forewarning of disaster. Then, suddenly, he heard a ferocious pounding and the tinkle of shattering glass.

Tucker whirled and saw one of Carry's followers hacking away at a cigar case with a hatchet. Carry and her second helpmate were hatcheting the bar, making chips fly in a manner that would have done credit to a burly lumberjack. Reacting to this assault, Tucker grabbed the house revolver and advanced on Carry. Undaunted, Carry aimed a sweeping hatchet stroke at his head. Tucker ducked, fortunately for him. Then he grabbed the wrist of the Amazon and wrenched the hatchet from her hand. Raising his gun, Tucker fired two warning shots into the rococo ceiling, and when these had no appreciable deterrent effect, he took to his heels, running out the rear door and shouting for the police.

Carry celebrated his flight by shouting, "For Your sake, Jesus!" Then she whipped out her spare hatchet from beneath the folds of her cape and went to work upon the large bar mirror.

Her two helpers were chopping away in fine frenzy, but they lacked Carry's imagination, ingenuity—and strength. Seeing the large cash register upon the bar, Carry grabbed it with both hands, wrenched the heavy thing from its base, raised it high above her head—and heaved. The force of her throw sent the machine halfway across the room, where it clattered to the floor, clanging "No Sale" and spraying bits and pieces of its mechanism, as well as its hoarded silver, onto the mounting pile of debris.

Next Carry swung the sharp edge of her hatchet against the rubber tube that carried beer from the tanks to the bar faucets. The severed tube acted like a hose, and Carry sprayed walls and ceilings with a cascade of malt that rained down like fine drops from heaven, drenching her and her followers. The Senate Bar was now a shambles, and it was just at this stage of the proceedings that police arrived upon the scene and led Carry gently away.

The law, as always, found Carry an embarrassment—but more so this time because the hatcheting of the Senate Bar fired the popular imagination. Instantaneously, Carry became a national figure. Cartoons showing her with her famous hatchet appeared in newspapers from coast to coast. Imitators sprang up, and throughout the state of Kansas women wielding hatchets went around wrecking bars. Some of their deeds rivaled those of Carry herself, but Carry, the innovator, remained in the public mind the Amazonian symbol of the anti-liquor campaign.

She toured the country on the lecture circuit, billed variously as the Home Defender, the Smasher, the Wrecker of Saloons. She published a weekly newspaper, *The Hatchet*. She even went to Washington and tried to see President Theodore Roosevelt to protest against the cigarette-smoking of his daughter, Alice, but the former Rough Rider of the Spanish-American War would have nothing to do with Carry Nation.

Gradually, as usually happens in cases of suddenly created mass hysteria, Carry's appeal faded. Though some members of the WCTU regarded her as a heroine of the cause, the organization itself turned against her with increasing hostility. The traditional American abhorrence of excessive violence began to assert itself, and by the time Carry suffered a stroke while speaking in Arkansas in January, 1911, she had become an irrelevant figure. She died on June 9, 1911, mourned by only a few of her most devoted followers.

Her saloon-smashing campaign, however, had not been in vain. She had helped focus public attention on the evil of excessive indulgence in alcohol, and she had paved the way for the more controlled fanatics of the Anti-Saloon League to capitalize on the widespread repugnance she had done so much to stimulate.

★

The first state branch of the Anti-Saloon League was organized in Ohio in 1893, and the national organization was formed two years later at a meeting in Washington, D.C. From the outset, the league's philosophy differed from that of temperance movements of the past. Its hard-boiled leaders realistically assessed the results of nearly a century of moral suasion and found them disappointing. In their view, the evil of liquor could be eliminated only by force. The answer lay in legislating the demon rum out of existence, and to accomplish this worthy end any pressure, any means, was justifiable.

A trade magazine, *The Wine and Spirit Circular*, early warned saloonkeepers of this new danger. It said:

"The Anti-Saloon League is not a mob of long-haired fanatics . . . but a strongly centralized organization, financed by capitalists with long purses, subscribed to by hundreds of thousands of men, women and children who are solicited by their various churches, advised by well-paid attorneys of great ability, and it is working with definite ideas to guide it in every state, in every county, in every city, in every precinct."

This was a perceptive description of the purposes of the league. It soon united all of the anti-liquor "temperance" groups under its banner. It formed a close working relationship with the WCTU. It had the almost complete cooperation of Protestant churches and appreciable support from many Jews and Catholics, and it was heavily backed financially by wealthy and powerful industrialists who had become convinced that drunkenness was a major menace in an era when machines demanded human speed-ups to achieve maximum mass production.

The man who welded all of these forces into the final, trium-

phant lobby of the temperance movement was a large, canny, ruthless
graduate of Oberlin College in Ohio—Wayne Bidwell Wheeler.
Wheeler had no sense of humor and little patience with human foibles.
He was a man with a mission, possessed, as one admiring friend said, by
"a passionate sincerity that bordered on unscrupulousness."

Wheeler became the league's superintendent and its congressional lobbyist. Virtually all the powers of the organization rested in his
hands. New initiatives originated with him, and he devised the ways and
means to make them acceptable to the public. According to Wheeler,
the league raised and spent in less than thirty years some $35 million "to
create and sustain public interest in its cause."

One of its creating and sustaining arms was the American Issue
Publishing Company in Westerville, Ohio, a propaganda organ that
turned out prohibitionist literature in great quantities. Another, more
covert branch of the organization consisted of a small army of field
agents working in states across the nation. The most illustrious of these
undercover men was William E. (Pussyfoot) Johnson, who recalled with
a rogue's pride how he had helped to get prohibition amendments
passed in several states. His task, he said, had been "publicity and
underground activities," and he explained that in this role he had drunk
"gallons of whiskey and told enough lies to make Ananias ashamed of
himself."

Wheeler's purpose was clear-cut: he aimed at achieving such
political influence that legislators backed by the Anti-Saloon League,
regardless of party, would constitute a bloc large enough to represent
the balance of power in state legislatures and in Congress itself. To this
end, those who agreed to vote "dry" must be supported—and those who
sided with the liquor interests must be defeated.

The effectiveness of Wheeler's methods was dramatically demonstrated in the 1904 gubernatorial campaign in Ohio. Governor M. T.
Herrick had infuriated the league by vetoing a local-option bill passed
by the legislature (a measure that would have permitted municipalities
to adopt ordinances banning the sale of liquor). Herrick argued that he
had had to veto the bill because he had made a promise to Mark Hanna,
the state and national Republican boss, the President-maker who had
put McKinley in the White House. Wheeler obtained a letter from
Hanna denying that he had ever required such a pledge from Herrick.

The Dry forces bombarded Republican leaders in an attempt to
prevent the renomination of Herrick, but the bosses backed the gover-

nor for reelection. So the Drys concentrated on the Democrats, who selected J. M. Pattison of Cincinnati, a supporter of the Anti-Saloon League.

The league's printing arm went into action and sent out 100,000 flyers urging the election of Pattison and branding Herrick a tool of the liquor interests. The governor denied the charge, but, unfortunately for him, the Fleischmann Distilling Company decided to "help him out" by distributing 75,000 copies of a laudatory pamphlet. On top of this, the Brewers Association urged its members to give employees time off on Election Day to work for Herrick.

With support like this tending to prove the charges of his opposition, the embattled governor hardly needed enemies. Copies of the Fleischmann broadside and the Brewers' letter fell into Wheeler's hands. "We got this on the Thursday before election," Wheeler later said, "photographed it and sent out thousands of copies to the churches on Sunday." The result: Herrick, who had been elected originally by a 100,000-vote margin, was defeated by 42,000 votes, running some 300,000 votes behind the popular national ticket headed by Teddy Roosevelt.

Such political pressure tactics began to dry up the nation, technically at least. State after state adopted prohibition laws. Georgia acted in 1907; North Carolina, Tennessee, Mississippi, West Virginia, and Oklahoma followed. Other states fell gradually into line, so that by the time the Anti-Saloon League held its annual convention in 1913, Wheeler could boast that "over two-thirds of the saloons of the nation are now in ten states."

To ban the demon rum from these ten obstinate citadels of inebriation, one final measure was needed—a national prohibition law. And Wheeler called for just such extreme action in his opening speech to the delegates.

"We welcome you . . . to the launching of the most beneficent and far-reaching movement since the Civil War," he told them. It was time "to march against the last bulwarks of the enemy." Voice soaring, he declaimed: "Like the muttering of a great storm you can hear the determined demand from every quarter to attack the enemy all along the line for National Constitutional Prohibition. I do not know how you may feel about this, but I would rather die than run from such a conflict."

The delegates felt about it just the way Wheeler must have

known in advance that they would. The league formed a committee of a thousand men, joined by a similar group of a thousand women from the WCTU, for a great march on Washington. The demonstration took place on December 10, 1913. Some four thousand men, women, and a few children, all wearing the white ribbon of temperance, paraded through the streets to the steps of the Capitol to the strains of "Onward, Christian Soldiers!"

An astute political manipulator, Wheeler staked everything on the election of 1916. He anticipated the reelection of President Woodrow Wilson, but, regardless of the outcome of the presidential contest, he was determined to secure the election of a Congress with enough committed Drys in it to assure passage of a prohibition amendment.

"Back in the field we got busy again," Wheeler said afterward. "We laid down such a barrage as candidates for Congress had never seen before. . . . We knew late election night that we had won. . . . We knew that the Prohibition Amendment would be submitted to the states by the Congress just elected."

World events now played into the hands of the man only too eager to use any cudgel to beat the hated foe. World War I was raging in Europe, and in April, 1917, the United States was drawn into the conflict. Wheeler at once seized the opportunity the war gave him to indulge in hysterical, superpatriotic rhetoric.

German-Americans were prominent in the brewing industry, and Wheeler's ploy was to link them and their product with the hated German enemy our doughboys were fighting. He equated Prohibition with patriotism. In a typical speech in Provincetown, Massachusetts, he declared:

"Kaiserism abroad and booze at home must go. . . . Liquor is a menace to patriotism because it puts beer before country. The shot and shell and poison gas of the Germans at the front are more easily met than insidious attacks in camp of the devils of lust, of gambling and of drink."

Ridiculous? Of course. But it had its effect. In the blind passions of the times, any person or deed marked with the faintest German taint was abhorred and repudiated.

Wheeler was determined to take full advantage of a moment that might never come again. His Anti-Saloon League had now pressured twenty-seven states into adopting Prohibition, and he reasoned that his cherished national amendment had to be passed by the Congress he had helped to elect. By 1920, after a new census, there would be a reapportionment of seats in the House of Representatives, and some forty new congressmen would come from the growing industrial areas where thirst was most acute.

With Wheeler lobbying and pressuring, and with his solid bloc of committed members in Congress, he got his wish. On August 1, 1917, the Senate passed the Eighteenth, or Prohibition, Amendment by a vote of 65 to 20, and the House followed on December 18, by 282 to 128. The amendment was swiftly ratified by the states on January 16, 1919, and a year later the nation became officially dry.

But only officially, only on the surface. Prohibition was what author Herbert Asbury has called the "Great Illusion." Americans, ordered not to drink, became determined to drink just as much as or more than ever. Defiance of the law became a national pastime in the profligate era of the Roaring Twenties. Bootlegging became a major national industry. Law enforcement and public officials were corrupted wholesale. Swaggering racketeers, backed by literally billions of illegal dollars, acquired an insidious money power that made them, in many instances, the real bosses of some of the nation's most powerful political machines.

A decade of this produced such national revulsion and disgust that Prohibition was repealed in 1933, but no mere turning back of the legislative clock could undo the damage. Many of the evils it fostered remain imbedded in American society: corruption on a scale more vast and more organized than anything that had existed previously, the continued flourishing of underworld cartels with billions of dollars derived from a variety of rackets, the infiltration of these illicit fortunes into broad sectors of legitimate American business. In addition, there are signs that, for some, the great illusion still persists.

On September 1, 1974, the Women's Christian Temperance Union held its one hundredth annual convention in Cleveland, Ohio. Some one thousand elderly women gathered in the Sheraton-Cleveland Hotel and sang the WCTU marching song, "Beverage Alcohol Must Go." It goes like this:

Save the nation.
Save the nation.
Join the fight against the deadly foe.

Save the nation.
Save the nation.
Beverage alcohol must go.

The WCTU still claims some 250,000 members, and its president, Mrs. Fred J. Tooze, seventy-one, delivered a rousing speech in which she claimed: "The thirteen years of Prohibition was [*sic*] one of the finest eras in the 200-year history of the United States."

The elderly delegates applauded that misinterpretation of history and vowed to continue their battle against all forms of the demon liquor. But they were living, as all the evidence indicates, in the nostalgia of the past. It is hardly likely that there will ever be another Carry Nation wielding a hatchet to break up saloons or that there will be another lobbyist like Wayne Wheeler exercising the kind of overwhelming political clout necessary to force through Congress an amendment dictating the drinking habits of Americans.

America's foreign policy, according to the Constitution, is supposed to be formulated by the President and the State Department, with the advice and consent of the Senate. But often, in actuality, the real decisions have been made, or forced upon the American people, by that so-called fourth branch of government—lobbyists working behind the scenes to determine official policy.

The most glaring example of the insidious role played by public relations men lobbying for a foreign client is to be found in the decades-long activity of what came to be known as the China Lobby. Its purpose was to make the American people deny an unpleasant reality—the fact that a Communist government ruled the most populous nation on earth—and to base American policy upon the illusion that the real and true government of China was represented by Generalissimo Chiang Kai-shek, who had been chased from the mainland and had holed up with his Nationalist forces on the offshore island of Formosa, now known as Taiwan.

So successful was the China Lobby that from 1949, when Chiang was forced from the mainland, until President Richard M. Nixon's precedent-setting visit to China in 1972, a period of twenty-three years, the United States refused to recognize the existence of the Chinese Communist regime, fought the admission of China to the United Nations, and placed all its bets on the fantasy that some day, somehow, Chiang would miraculously return to the mainland and reestablish his rule.

6

THE CHINA LOBBY

This policy made no sense, not even to some of the highest American officials who were committed to it. Clayton Fritchey, who served as an aide to Ambassador Adlai Stevenson at the United Nations, once wrote: "John F. Kennedy frankly told his top associates that he thought U.S. China policy was 'irrational.' Most of them agreed with him; and many senior officials of the Johnson Administration felt the same way. . . . Still, when the chips were down, these Administrations backed away from any change."

Such was the power and influence of the China Lobby.

The lobby went through several stages, using various front men, but much of its activity was financed by Chiang himself, often with the help of the hundreds of millions of dollars the United States had given him to support his regime. It was one of the neatest ploys in history—our own money being used to finance our own brainwashing.

The propaganda effort began even while Chiang's regime was supposed to be our partner in World War II. From the outset, American official attitudes toward China had been marked by illusory, wishful thinking. This huge Asian land mass with its teeming population (now nearly 800 million people) was not a unified nation. Invaded by the Japanese in the 1930s, torn internally by the incessant warring of avaricious warlords, China represented chaos. Chiang had emerged as the most powerful of the warlords, but there was little justification for magnifying him into a national leader on a par with Winston Churchill, Joseph Stalin, and Franklin D. Roosevelt.

Nevertheless, in hope and need, the Roosevelt administration envisioned Chiang as the messiah who would create a mighty nation to rank with Great Britain, the Soviet Union, and the United States. And so we committed ourselves wholly to Chiang as our ally in the war against Japan. We strengthened his forces with $825.7 million in Lend Lease aid, and we supported his regime with $645 million in cash loans. Of the latter amount, $500 million was in a Treasury gold shipment over which we exercised no control, and, as a consequence, much of this was sold on the Chinese black market. Treasury Secretary Henry Morgenthau reported to President Roosevelt in December, 1943, that "such schemes in the past have had little effect except to give additional profits to insiders, speculators and hoarders." The identity of these fortunate profiteers was never clearly established, but persistent and seemingly creditable reports indicated they were members of Chiang's inner circle.

Skillful in the ways of corruption Chiang's palace guards certainly were, but fighting tigers they were not. General Joseph (Vinegar Joe) Stillwell almost went out of his mind trying to get Chiang's troops to fight the Japanese invaders. But Chiang preferred to hoard most of the military aid we gave him for the eventual showdown with his Chinese Communist foes, led by Mao Tse-tung. As a result, the Japanese forged deep into China, driving Chiang into the hinterlands before American forces won the war for him.

In the postwar era, Chiang rapidly lost control of China. There was a split even within his own dominant Kuomintang party, with Chiang stepping down from the presidency on January 21, 1949. From that time on, there were in effect two squabbling factions instead of what was supposed to be a united front against the Communists.

The collapse of Chiang in China coincided with a political shocker in the United States—the reelection of President Harry S. Truman in the 1948 campaign in which Republican Governor Thomas E. Dewey of New York had been supposed to be unbeatable. Chiang had banked heavily on Dewey's election as the harbinger of more massive American aid, and he was alarmed by the Truman administration's cool reassessment of the turmoil in China. In this exigency, Madame Chiang came to Washington to mastermind the reorganization and expansion of Chiang's lobbying apparatus. When Chiang was chased from the mainland in December, 1949, a calculated campaign began to blame the United States—and by implication traitors at the highest level of the American government—for "the loss of China."

In the anti-Communist hysteria of the time, the most obvious fact failed to register on the American mind—that China had been Chiang's, not ours, to lose. This is a tribute to one of the most massive and successful foreign lobbying campaigns in American history, an effort that benefited from a conjunction of events both foreign and domestic. On the home front, many Republican orators, made almost paranoid by the stunning upset of 1948, were ready to use any stick, even the irresponsible charge of treason against Truman himself, with which to beat their Democratic foes. Abroad, the outbreak of the Korean War in 1950, with Chinese Communists fighting against our troops in North Korea, convinced many that there *had* to be some devil's work afoot. Otherwise, how explain a world gone suddenly awry after the sweeping, heady triumph of 1945?

Max Ascoli, then editor of *The Reporter*, described how all of these factors united to promote the China Lobby. In an introduction to a two-part series on the lobby (April 15, 1952), he wrote:

"The fall of China invigorated . . . a partnership between Chinese and American factions eagerly involved in the politics of each other's country. The Chinese partners are the agents of a government that can rule China again only if the United States destroys Mao's forces in an all-out war. The American partners are an ill-assorted lot—honest men deeply concerned with the plight of the Chinese people and of Chiang Kai-shek; fanatics possessed by the nightmare of a Communist conspiracy centering on some of America's highest leaders; and politicians who will stop at nothing in their hunt for power.

"This partnership of Chinese-American fear, ambition and greed is the China Lobby. . . ."

It might have been more accurate to say that this partnership formed the basis of support for the China Lobby, for the lobby itself took more tangible forms. It worked its will through a succession of public relations maneuvers that forced the United States to deny for more than twenty years the reality of who wielded power in China—and who didn't. One of the most remarkable feats that promoted a mirage into reality was the creation of the Committee of One Million Against the Admission of Communist China to the United Nations, or, as it became known (that title being too unwieldy), the Committee of One Million.

Actually, there was no "committee of one million." The "committee" consisted of little more than a lone public relations man and a few helpers. The promotional genius was Marvin Liebman, who operated out of an office at 343 Lexington Avenue, New York City, and whose fertile mind transformed a million ghosts into a power accepted by the American press and public as a reality.

What Liebman did was simple beyond belief: in 1953 and 1954, with the wounds of Korea fresh in the public mind, he concocted the idea of getting a million Americans to sign a petition opposing the admission of Communist China to the United Nations. In the mood of the times, as he later said, "anyone would have signed the petition then." And so, according to Liebman's count, at least, 1,037,000 Americans signed—and then the petitions were packed away in a New York warehouse, untouched by human hand, mute paper symbols of what Liebman trumpeted as the national mood.

How did this myth of a million-member "committee" develop?

In 1953, with the Korean War winding down, there was growing pressure from some of America's allies, especially Great Britain, for the adoption of a more realistic attitude toward Red China. After all, China *did* exist—and it was not Taiwan. Britain argued for recognition of the Communist regime as indisputably the actual ruler of China and for the relaxation of the American-proclaimed trade embargo. The Stockholm Peace Appeal, soon to be denounced as a Communist-front endeavor, claimed to have obtained the signatures of 11 million Americans to petitions advocating China's admission to the United Nations.

In protest against such heresy, Liebman embarked on his first public relations campaign in October, 1953. He got 212 politicians, businessmen, scientists, and religious leaders to sign a statement urging that China still be considered unfit to associate with civilized nations. President Dwight D. Eisenhower was on his way to a Bermuda conference with British leaders, and this original statement was given to the President "to arm you in speaking to the British."

More "arming," however, obviously was needed. A mere 212 names in opposition to 11 million was not very impressive, and so Liebman and some of his original signers decided they must round up the signatures of at least one million.

"Congressional signers [of the original statement] got mail both pro and con," Liebman later acknowledged, but he insisted that "before we knew it there was a spontaneous movement."

Just how "spontaneous" the movement was seems open to question. Even Liebman acknowledged that signatures came in slowly, but he explained that there were inevitable delays because support had to be obtained from a number of cooperating organizations. These included the American Legion, the American Federation of Labor, the Benevolent and Protective Order of Elks, the General Federation of Women's Clubs, and the Catholic War Veterans.

With such assistance, Liebman and his small hard core of supporters (which included the honorary chairman of the committee, Warren R. Austin, a former U.S. senator and our first ambassador to the United Nations) dispatched a wire to President Eisenhower on September 9, 1954, declaring that they had rounded up their million signers. Neither the text of the petition nor the presumably long scroll of signers went to the White House. All of this validating evidence was simply deposited in a warehouse, where it ticked away like some hidden time bomb menacing the American political scene.

Ironically, the 11 million signatures gathered by the Stockholm Peace Appeal were dismissed by the State Department as Russian-inspired fakery, but those million names hidden in warehouse darkness were accepted as the bona-fide expression of American will. Public officials and newspaper editors across the land took the Committee of One Million at face value, and its statements were treated with the respect that would naturally be accorded to an organization representing the sentiments (as Liebman claimed) of 95 percent of the American people.

Even some outstanding and generally independent political leaders swallowed the one-million propaganda whole. Foremost among these were two respected Democratic senators—Mike Mansfield, of Montana, a former professor of political science and now majority leader, and Paul H. Douglas, of Illinois, long known as a battler for the causes of the average man. "What is *he* doing there?" was a question often asked about Douglas. The answer seems to be that Douglas, like Mansfield, honestly believed the representations of the Committee of One Million.

Mansfield, indeed, once asserted that the committee represented many additional millions because its stand had been endorsed by many national organizations. "Americans who favor the admission of Red China to the United Nations base part of their argument on the false premise that opposition to such admission comes from a minority and lunatic conservative fringe of American politics," he said.

He obviously accepted without question Liebman's claim that his committee expressed the "grass roots sentiments of all America." Yet, out of the million Americans supposed to be on the "committee," not more than six thousand ever contributed so much as a dime, and no more than twenty-five thousand ever appeared on the committee's mailing list.

With the passage of time, world conditions changed drastically. Tensions built up between China and Russia; border warfare between the two seemed likely to erupt at almost any moment; and it became obvious that the Communist world was not one united front but had its own nationalistic interests and rivalries. It also became more and more apparent that Chiang, with his relative handful of followers, would never be able to reestablish his rule over the hundreds of millions on the mainland. Yet the Committee of One Million held to its original objectives as if no changes had occurred in the world, and American politics was locked into the rigidity the committee did so much to foster.

Each new threat to cherished beliefs spurred new activity by the committee. In the fall of 1954 an assembly of Protestant religious leaders seemed to be leaning toward the recognition of China, and Liebman's group responded with new lobbying activity. No effort was made to see whether any of the original signers of the warehouse petition might have had second thoughts. "It would have been too expensive," Liebman explained. And so the committee of one million ghosts continued to harass the American political scene.

Typical of its tactics was a headline-catching letter it dispatched early in 1962 to U.N. Ambassador Adlai Stevenson, the representative of the skeptical Kennedy administration. In this communiqué the committee thundered that "continued American support of the U. N." would not be possible "if the Charter is weakened and ultimately destroyed" through the recognition and admission of China to the world council. The handout claimed that this position had the support of 55 U.S. senators and 294 members of the House of Representatives, a majority of both houses of Congress.

Publisher W. E. Chilton, III, of the *Charleston Gazette* in West Virginia looked at the list of names and began to doubt. Many whose support the committee claimed were liberals who, it seemed, would be unlikely to take so dogmatic a stand. Skeptical, Chilton decided to send out a questionnaire testing the validity of the committee's claim.

He asked four questions: Were you consulted in advance about whether you agreed with the statement of the Committee of One Million? Are you consulted in advance about the public positions the committee takes? What role do congressional endorsers play in shaping committee policy? Do you believe the United States should stop supporting the U.N. if Communist China is admitted?

Chilton got twenty-five replies to the fifty letters he sent out. Only two of his correspondents, Senator Douglas and Senator Kenneth Keating (Republican, New York), said they had been consulted in advance about the committee's statement. And Douglas said he had *flatly refused* to sign the open letter to Ambassador Stevenson—yet the committee had gone right ahead and used his name.

Other replies exposed the committee's claim that it had majority support in Congress. Speaker of the House John W. McCormack (Democrat, Massachusetts) declared he was resigning from the committee. He explained that he opposed the admission of Communist China, but that he disagreed with many of the committee's policy statements.

Still others whose support the committee had claimed made it clear that, while they might oppose the admission of China, they were equally opposed to destroying the United Nations by having America withdraw over the issue. This group included senators Douglas, Clinton P. Anderson (Democrat, New Mexico), Mike Monroney (Democrat, Oklahoma), Thurston B. Morton (Republican, Kentucky), Stuart Symington (Democrat, Missouri), Jennings Randolph (Democrat, West Virginia), and representatives John D. Dingell (Democrat, Michigan) and James G. Fulton (Republican, Pennsylvania).

Three others who had been listed as members of the "committee" insisted that they weren't and never had been. Senators Clifford P. Chase (Republican, New Jersey) and Leverett Saltonstall (Republican, Massachusetts) said that they had signed the original petition circulated by Liebman, but that they hadn't endorsed any subsequent statements and certainly didn't consider themselves committee members. Even more remarkable was the statement of Representative James C. Wright (Democrat, Texas), who said, "I have never heard of the so-called 'Committee of One Million' prior to the receipt of your letter. . . . I have emphatically not signed or agreed to any such statement as that quoted in your letter."

When a congressman who hadn't even heard of the committee was cited by it as an endorser of its policies, little more need be said about the credence that should have been given to its statements. Yet the American press as a whole had accepted the committee's handout as if it reflected the bona fide attitudes of Congress and the American people.

The Committee of One Million flourished for years and wielded amazing influence, but it was not the only arm of the China Lobby. A far more sophisticated and subtle propaganda operation, one that pulled much of the complacent American media around by the nose, was directly financed by Chiang in an effort to brainwash the American people—and through them to influence Congress—into believing that his Nationalist regime had a real chance of resuming its rule over all of China.

This part of the China Lobby story was dragged into the light in

1963 when Senator J. William Fulbright (Democrat, Arkansas), chairman of the Senate Foreign Relations Committee, held a series of hard-digging hearings to determine just how much of our foreign policy is our own creation—and how much is the product of deliberate distortion and lobbying by agents in the pay of foreign governments.

In the China Lobby phase of his hearings, Fulbright focused a glaring spotlight on the activities of Hamilton Wright, one of the largest, wealthiest, and most influential public relations agencies in America. He disclosed that the Hamilton Wright Organization, camouflaging propaganda as legitimate news, had infiltrated the American media on a broad scale on behalf of Chiang Kai-shek and the apartheid government of the Union of South Africa. It also, incidentally, handled a tourism account for Mexico, and this sometimes came in handy in granting special favors to media representatives who could reciprocate by treating gently HWO's Chiang–South Africa efforts. It was a three-way package that was tied together like a thing of beauty.

The Hamilton Wright Organization became devoted to Chiang in 1957, and its love affair with the dictator of Taiwan flourished at a stipend of $300,000 a year through 1962. From the outset, the agency's role was clear: it proposed to sell the American people a bill of goods on a colossal scale.

The methods and objectives were set forth in a letter sent on May 2, 1957, to Dr. T. F. Tsiang, Chiang's representative at the U.N. The public relations agency made it clear that it saw Chiang's island empire as one of the great dramatic stories of the times—that it represented the establishment, nurturing, and growth of a new "free" nation. To tell this story in words and pictures, Hamilton Wright proposed to send "our own crew of experts" to Taiwan, where "we would research, *create and manufacture news*" (emphasis added).

This creation and manufacturing of news had a clear-cut purpose: "As you well know, every Senator, Representative, politician—even our President—is first, last and always . . . the servant of the American people. . . .

"To inform the voters—to make them Free China-conscious—to make the American people aware of the tremendous uphill fight the 10 million Chinese have won on Taiwan—to get across the 'human interest' story—is the first step toward these objectives."

In accepting HWO's proposal, Chiang made his motives clear.

His Government Information Office, in a letter to HWO on August 9, 1957, put it bluntly:

"The 'two Chinas' theory has never been totally discredited. There have been talks of admitting the Chinese Communists in the United Nations, of relaxing the embargo of strategic material to the Chinese mainland, and of taking another look at U.S. policy toward China.

"It is for this reason that we want to avoid creating the impression that the building up of Taiwan is an end in itself, that the Government is content with just sitting here, and that we have given up the goal of returning to the mainland."

In pursuit of Chiang's impossible dream, the Hamilton Wright boys knocked themselves out in operations virtually global in scope. Their far-ranging plans embraced whole continents, as Hamilton Wright himself made clear in a 1959 letter to Dr. Sampson Shen, director of Chiang's Government Information Office.

Wright proposed nothing less than a massive campaign through all of South America in 1960 because "these countries have twenty-one votes in the United Nations" and keeping them in Chiang's camp would help to freeze out Communist China. HWO's color motion picture *The Face of Free China* would be given a Spanish sound track for distribution in South and Central America. So would a companion film, *Majestic Island,* for which "professional distribution" was being arranged with Universal-International pictures. American news services to South America would be fed favorable stories. Arrangements were being made with the U.S. Information Service "to push HWO movies, newsreels and shorts wherever possible in South America."

There were plans for a new color motion picture, *Taiwan—Asian Showcase.* Hamilton Wright wrote flatly: "Metro-Goldwyn-Mayer will distribute this picture: we have already discussed with MGM the theatrical distribution of this picture. They have agreed to give it widespread circulation in most Middle East, Southeast Asian, and Latin American countries under the title '*MGM Presents, etc.*' (*and not as a picture earmarked 'Government of China,' etc.*)" (emphasis added).

In all of this global "think," the United States was not to be neglected. Wright declared: "The U.S. publicity must continue hard and en masse, reaching further and deeper into thought leaders, political thinking, and to the American people. Grassroots publicity is priceless." Wright believed that the time was right to invade the largest mass circulation magazines—"*Saturday Evening Post, Reader's Digest, Life, Look, Redbook, McCall's, Time, Newsweek, etc.*" He also reported that "this year we were successful in getting cooperation in this direction which resulted in signed articles being published in leading newspapers (see scrapbooks). More can be done. More will be done."

To further this "more can, more will" proposition, Wright cooked up his own "impartial" expert, a man whose skill and manufactured status made it possible for him to infiltrate the columns of the largest newspapers. In a subsequent memo, Wright described this development:

"Last year Ambassador George Yeh said to me, 'Ham, I think your organization should develop a man who can become an authority on China. One who knows us, our way of life, our problems, a man who can write with complete understanding.' After two years we believe that our Don Frifield is now that man. He is regarded by the U. S. newspapers as a top authority on China problems. In order not to appear as a 'propaganda' outlet for Free China, we have arranged for Don to write on many subjects on the Far East, Japan, the Philippines, Korea, etc. This gives depth and recognition to his work and opens the way to penetrate with publicity on Free China."

In questioning the Wrights, father and son, Fulbright's committee demonstrated how one arm of the China Lobby helped the other. Frifield's articles, pure paid-for propaganda for Chiang, were funneled to the Committee of One Million, which then used its peculiar prestige to get congressmen and senators to agree to have the stories printed under their names as if they themselves had written them.

Senator Douglas was one victim of this devious ploy. He had approved the use of his name as the by-line author for one of Frifield's articles in June, 1959. But he had had no idea, Douglas told Fulbright's committee, that the article had been created by a hired hand for Chiang Kai-shek.

"I was informed that the manuscript had been prepared by the Hamilton Wright Organization," Senator Douglas wrote, "but I was not informed that this company was in receipt of any retainer from the Chinese Nationalist Government itself and have insisted that the Committee of One Million should not receive any direct or indirect subvention from it. . . . I have remained on the Committee of One

Million's executive committee only on the assurance that no direct or indirect financing came from the Nationalist Chinese Government and that the committee was independently financed."

If the fine hand of Chiang was so well hidden that even a U.S. senator couldn't sense it in an article ghosted for him, there was little chance that the ordinary magazine reader or casual theatergoer would suspect that what he was reading or seeing was not an impartial and factual report but subtle brainwashing propaganda.

This issue was one that greatly concerned Fulbright and his committee, and Fulbright himself delved deeply into it in questioning Hamilton Wright, Sr. Wright had displayed a full page of pictures extolling the beauties of South Africa that had appeared in the Washington *Star*, one of the capital's two great newspapers.

FULBRIGHT: Are you responsible for this?

WRIGHT, SR.: Our name is on the bottom there, "Photos Hamilton Wright."

FULBRIGHT: Does it say there, "Agent for the South African Government?"

WRIGHT, SR.: Well, they know it was from South Africa. It doesn't say that, no paper publishes that.

FULBRIGHT: Do the people who read it know it? Would I know it by reading that?

The discussion continued, with Fulbright finally saying:

FULBRIGHT: Your proposition is that you have no responsibility for its being identified when actually published, is that correct?

WRIGHT, SR.: That is correct. In other words, here is a CinemaScope picture released by Twentieth Century-Fox on South Africa which we produced. At no time is there any question in the mind of Twentieth Century-Fox that this—that the people who produced this picture, namely the Hamilton Wright Organization, were made to do it by the Government of South Africa. But you cannot ask Twentieth Century-Fox for them to go out and say this is publicity released by the Hamilton Wright Organization and paid for by the Government of South Africa.

FULBRIGHT: Why can't you?

WRIGHT, SR.: They won't do it.

FULBRIGHT: It seems to me that is what the law requires.

WRIGHT, SR.: You would have to go to Twentieth Century-Fox and ask
    them to do it. By the way, if a man goes to a theater, if you go to
    Radio City Music Hall, and ask them to run a piece of propa-
    ganda on the screen, they would revolt at it. You wouldn't pay to
    go in . . . to see a piece of propaganda.
FULBRIGHT: That is actually what is happening, isn't it?
WRIGHT, SR.: Well—
FULBRIGHT: The only difference is that you just don't tell them that.

How did HWO, which was being paid $300,000 annually by
Chiang and $150,000 by the Union of South Africa, manage to palm off
propaganda as legitimate news? The Fulbright investigation suggested
some possible answers, all traceable to a basic principle of the huckster:
"One hand washes the other."

When Hamilton Wright produced a color film on the glories of
Taiwan, he naturally needed an expert cameraman. So he hired Richard
Kuhne at $250 a week. And who was Richard Kuhne? The son of Jack
Kuhne, in charge of Twentieth Century-Fox's short subjects.

A few years later, Wright found himself able to give a helping
hand to another son of Jack Kuhne—Robert. On April 6, 1962, he wrote
Robert Kuhne about shooting a 16 mm. short for HWO on the glories
of Mexico:

"I had lunch with your dad yesterday—and you might also like to
know that we sent you a check for three weeks' advance—$1,800—that's
what we think of Bob Kuhne."

Having exposed the nature of HWO's ties to Twentieth Century-Fox, the Fulbright committee turned to Metro-Goldwyn-Mayer,
the great film company that had distributed a number of HWO short
subjects and newsreel shots. Max Klein was editor of the MGM newsreel, and correspondence showed that he enjoyed an especially warm
and close relationship with Hamilton Wright, Sr. One Klein note found
in the HWO files dealt with a junket to Mexico that was being arranged
for him by Wright. Klein wrote:

"The idea of winging down Mexico way as the (honored) guest
of the Government appeals to me—and the wife, of course. . . . Again,
Ham, arranging this trip is not a requisite for our continued friendship.
We are much too close to allow anything or anyone, to interfere with
that. By the way, I intend to keep this sub rosa . . . it is best for all
concerned."

The Klein junket led to this discussion between Fulbright and Wright, Sr.:

FULBRIGHT: In effect, this is the way you pay Mr. Klein for releasing your shorts.

WRIGHT, SR.: No. How do you mean payment?

FULBRIGHT: Just what I mean.

WRIGHT, SR.: No. We don't pay him anything. This is a courtesy. This is a courtesy that is commonly extended to editors of the working press all the years I have been in business. . . . This doesn't mean he has to accept your material when you give it to him. He can still reject it, and he rejects a lot of our material because some of it isn't up to par.

FULBRIGHT: It says he has released all the newsreels.

WRIGHT, SR.: This is good. He hasn't rejected them because they are good newsreels. Is there anything wrong with this? Is there something wrong with this?

That, said Fulbright, was exactly what he was trying to find out.

His inquiry showed that the Mexican tourism account afforded Wright the opportunity to do little favors, which presumably would be appreciated, for a number of important media executives. Louis Messolonghetis, an editor of King Features, the Hearst chain's major syndication outlet, junketed to Mexico under an arrangement similar to Klein's. So did Courtland Smith, an editor of Central Press Association, a division of King Features. So did Jack Woliston, a news editor of United Press Association. Harold Blumenthal, picture editor of UPI, was the beneficiary of "many trips" to Puerto Rico.

Courtland Smith fairly bubbled his gratitude in a letter written to Hamilton Wright, Sr., on December 7, 1960:

"The suite at the Hilton was lavish and we had fine accommodations at the Victoria in Taxco and the Coleta in Acapulco. . . . You told me the government would pick up the full tab, so we signed for everything at the Hilton, including the Cook's tour."

Fulbright, citing Smith's letter, asked Wright, Sr., "You do not think this has any bearing upon the objectivity or independence of the news and pictures disseminated by the Central Press Association?" In reply, Wright protested that "you come to a point now where do you stop and start in doing business with people?" It was a question he asked—but didn't answer.

Against this background of favors granted and material published, Wright's proudest achievement—his creation of the "impartial
expert," Don Frifield—deserves closer attention. Wright seemed in-
sulted at a published report that he had paid Frifield a mere $18,000 a
year. The price, he said, was $25,000. In return, Frifield turned out
articles that were submitted "to North American Newspaper Alliance,
to other syndicates, to newspapers direct, Sunday newspapers, on the
basis of being free, and they could reject or accept them. . . . They
published a tremendous lot and requested more articles."

Fulbright asked whether Frifield's articles carried a label identi-
fying them as paid propaganda. Yes, said Wright, the articles definitely
carried such a label when they were mailed to distant newspapers;
perhaps not when they were sent to editors in New York with whom he
had close personal relations. These editors, he explained, knew the
score. He said that the New York *Herald-Tribune* (one of the city's
great newspapers, now defunct) "absolutely" knew of Frifield's connection because "I have many friends over there."

FULBRIGHT: Do you know whether Mr. Frifield was paid by the *Her-
      ald-Tribune* for these articles?
WRIGHT, SR.: He may have been paid, just to make a token payment for
      stories that had nothing to do with the client. It may have been a
      token payment on a story on the refugees in Hong Kong.

Wright explained that the Hong Kong refugee stories, which for
some months were a *Herald-Tribune* favorite, originated with HWO.
He clearly felt it was one of the scoops of the year. One of the first stories
dealt with two boys who had floated on basketballs "across 1,600 feet of
water to Quemoy," a small offshore island. Wire services interviewed
them, Wright said, "and they exposed living conditions in Communist
China. They showed the tremendous handicap the people were living
under, and it all pointed up that the democratic way of life is a whole lot
better than the Communist way of life, and this was a link, our getting
ahead of this story and opening it up to editors was a link that resulted
in many magazine stories, many Sunday feature stories."

It was a performance that also helped to foster the delusion that
all China was trying to escape to Hong Kong or other non-Communist
areas and that the Communist regime on the mainland must be on the
point of virtual collapse. American policy clung to this bit of wishful
thinking for years, and so did many Americans who, like Hamilton

Wright, had no conception of Chinese realities. To picture Chiang as the representative of "the democratic way of life" was to indulge in idiotic fantasy. Chiang had been a brutal dictator, and conditions under his regime had been so horrible that all the Chinese people had been offered was a choice between dictatorships: between the one they knew that offered them only misery and degradation, and the one they didn't know that, just possibly, might give them something better.

This reality, this limited choice, was understood by some who had lived in the China of Chiang, and they spoke for sanity. But their voices were drowned out by the overwhelming propaganda chorus orchestrated by the Committee of One Million and the Hamilton Wright Organization.

For example, John O'Kearney, a former Far Eastern correspondent for the New York *Daily News,* writing in *The Nation,* described Liebman's "admitted" and "absolute" ignorance "of the evils of Kuomintang rule" when "every dawn [in Shanghai] revealed more than a hundred human bodies to be carted off out of the filth of the gutters." Han Suyin, author of the best-selling *A Many-Splendored Thing,* recalled on one *Today* telecast some of the incredible hardships of Chinese life during this same period. It was common, she said, for an entire family to possess only a single blanket under which all had to huddle in an attempt to keep warm. It was common for the males of a family to have only one suit among them—and when one went out to work, wearing the one suit, the others had to hide at home in nakedness. At least under Communist rule, she said, each man in a family had something with which to clothe himself—and, miracle of miracles, *a telephone* had actually been installed in the block in which she once had lived. Needless to say, this kind of essential backgrounding, without which there could be no understanding of what was happening in China, did not find its way into the paid propaganda articles, masquerading as news, that flooded the American press.

Reality, of course, can be denied only so long. As years stretched into decades, it became obvious that America's favorite policy rationalization—the belief that Chinese communism was about to collapse from internal pressures, from the revolt of the people—was a delusion. Other nations in the world, less blinkered by anti-Communist phobia, recognized this long before we did; and throughout the decade of the 1960s, pressures steadily mounted in the United Nations to recognize the regime that indisputably held sway over mainland China.

The United States delegations to the U.N., whatever might have been the private feelings of the Kennedy and Johnson administrations, were locked into rigid opposition. By 1971, however, it became apparent that, lacking the support of many of our own allies, the battle to exclude the most populous nation on earth from U.N. deliberations could be waged no longer. An effort was then made to save face by adopting the very "two-China" policy against which Chiang and the Committee of One Million had inveighed so mightily. During all the years of the U.N.'s existence, Chiang had held China's seat as if he really represented China. And so, finally yielding to the inevitable, the United States said, in effect, "Seat Communist China if you must, we will support that; but don't throw out Chiang."

It was now too late for such a compromise, however. On October 25, 1971, the U.N. General Assembly voted to seat Communist China, and, at the same time, it expelled Chiang's Taiwan regime.

This action was followed by President Nixon's unprecedented visit to China, February 21–28, 1972. Ironically, in the political wars of the 1950s, Nixon had been one of the foremost political criers of alarm about the Communist menace. His had been one of the strongest voices in the land in denouncing anyone who suggested the possibility of normal diplomatic relationships with Communist countries. Yet now, as President, it was Nixon who opened up a dialogue with Communist China. This first overture was followed by each country's opening liaison offices in the other's capital and by the resumption of trade with China—a boon to American businessmen, who sold more goods to China in 1974, especially foodstuffs, than they did to the Soviet Union, with which we had long maintained commercial ties.

If Nixon's about-face shocked many of his right-wing followers, it must be said that he was not the only politician to change with changing times. December, 1974, found Senator Mike Mansfield—another who had uncritically accepted the claims of the Committee of One Million twenty years earlier—visiting China's capital of Peking and assuring Chinese leaders that the new American attitude toward China was "irreversible."

The China Lobby had kept its finger in the dike for nearly twenty years, but the realities of life in the end had overcome it.

Among dates to remember one should perhaps keep in mind February 20, 1966. It is as good a time as any at which to pinpoint the emergence of something new on the American scene, the birth of the so-called people's lobbies.

Granted, there was no sudden, visible act of creation on that February 20, but what happened then was a beginning, the kind of striking and unusual event that helps to make the unprecedented happen —and keep right on happening.

The scene was this: a neighborhood drugstore near Dupont Circle in Washington, D.C. A young man, six feet, four inches tall, with an angular face, thick black hair, and black bushy eyebrows, was flipping through the latest magazines on the store rack. As he was so occupied, a striking young brunette came striding into the store and walked directly up to him.

"I know this sounds forward," she said in a seductive voice, "but can I talk to you?"

The handsome young man's jaw fell open. He was not accustomed to the direct siren approach.

Evidently mistaking his astonishment for interest, the confident young brunette explained that she and some of her friends were discussing "foreign affairs" in a nearby apartment. Would the young man like to join them?

This was certainly one of the most novel gambits in the history of intrigue. One look at the curvaceous charmer would have convinced almost any male that certain affairs might very well be discussed with her. But "foreign affairs"?

7

THE PEOPLE'S LOBBIES

Nonplussed by the suggestion, the tall young man stammered, as he later recalled, something to the effect: "I'm a stranger here from out-of-town. I haven't the time."

A bit huffy at this cold rejection of her freewill offering, the brunette swung around on one high heel and walked out of the store without attempting to recruit any of the other male customers for her "foreign affairs" discussion.

The incident with the mysterious brunette was duplicated two days later when an equally well-stacked and mysterious blonde swayed into the young man's ken. This time, he was in a Safeway supermarket near his Washington boardinghouse. It was evening, and shoppers filled the aisles. The young man was in the section marked "cookies," trying to decide what to buy, when the tall blonde in slacks swept down the aisle and came directly up to him.

"I need some help," she said without preamble. "I've got to move something heavy into my apartment. There's no one to help me. I wonder if I can get you to give me a hand. It won't take much time. Will you help?"

Poor, helpless, pathetic, beautiful blonde. What red-blooded male could resist going to her rescue? Well, this particular young male could. No, he told the blonde flatly, he wouldn't help her. She persisted, trying to wheedle him, but he turned his back on her. And the blonde, just like the brunette before her, wheeled around and stalked out of the store without trying to enlist the help of any of the other available young males in the place.

The young man who had proved himself so impervious to the wiles of both blonde and brunette was Ralph Nader, who, thanks to these and other shady maneuvers, was soon to become the hero of much of America—and the common man's most persistent and effective consumer advocate.

At the time, Nader was locked in a fierce, no-holds-barred struggle with General Motors, the dominant automobile manufacturer and one of the most powerful corporations in America. Nader, a young Connecticut lawyer of Lebanese ancestry, had written a book, *Unsafe at Any Speed*, that was a blistering indictment of America's car-makers. Nader's basic thesis was that Detroit was producing chrome-plated, flashy vehicles that became virtual deathtraps in collisions—sometimes even at such ridiculously low speeds as fifteen miles an hour.

His denunciation of the profit-oriented, safety-be-damned attitude of Detroit had spared no one, but General Motors had been
especially gored. Nader had charged that GM's new compact, the Corvair—an innovation in American cars with its engine in the rear—was one
of the most dangerous cars ever built. Corvairs were so unstable, he
wrote, that they sometimes flipped over rounding a curve in a crosswind
at even moderate speed, and he cited cases in which the occupants of
such Corvairs had been either maimed or killed.

Nader's charges against the Corvair had been given wide publicity, not just in his book but in magazines as well. *The Nation*, with its
small but influential circulation, had excerpted the Corvair chapter for
an issue in November, 1965. Reviews, when they appeared in the nation's press, had focused on the Corvair charges and praised Nader's
careful documentation. And Nader himself had carried his case to the
public in speeches and television appearances. All of this came at an
especially bad time for GM. The huge auto firm was faced with 106
lawsuits, seeking $40 million in damages, brought by owners of 1960–63
Corvairs who had experienced the kind of road disasters Nader had
described.

This was the situation when an article in the Sunday *New York
Times* on March 6, 1966, triggered the next act in the drama. The story
appeared on page 94 of the *Times'* second section; it spread across eight
columns; and the headline read: CRITIC OF AUTO INDUSTRY'S SAFETY
STANDARDS SAYS HE WAS TRAILED AND HARASSED: CHARGE CALLED ABSURD.

Among the readers of the *Times* on this fateful day was James
Roche, president of GM. The article that he read charged that Nader,
who was appearing before a traffic safety subcommittee headed by
Senator Abraham Ribicoff (Democrat, Connecticut), was being spied
upon and harassed in what appeared to be an effort by someone in the
auto industry to intimidate him. It quoted Nader as saying that he was
being disturbed by late-night telephone calls; that men, apparently
private detectives, had trailed him right into the corridors of the New
Senate Office Building; and that women had been used as lures in a
transparent effort to lead him into some compromising trap. There was
no indication of the identity of the auto firm that might be behind such
underhanded activities, but since Nader had focused so strongly on the
deficiencies of the Corvair, suspicion fell almost automatically on GM.
Roche, reading the account, felt a premonitory tremor and began to

make a series of telephone calls to determine whether GM actually was involved.

Roche's inquiries at first drew a blank. GM's legal and public relations staffs in Washington insisted they knew nothing about anyone harassing Nader. Satisfied, Roche on Tuesday instructed GM's public relations department in New York to issue a flat denial that his corporation had had anything to do with the "alleged" surveillance of Nader. Then, before the statement could be issued, the roof caved in on Jim Roche.

He later testified: "In the process of ordering a formal statement denying our involvement, I discovered to my dismay that we were indeed involved."

GM's public relations motors had to be thrown into reverse at the last second. After infinite thrashing about in the executive suite, GM finally issued a statement on March 9, 1966, that admitted "the office of its general counsel initiated a routine investigation through a reputable law firm" to determine whether Nader's published attacks on the Corvair were linked to suits for damages being brought by owners of that unstable vehicle.

"It is a well-known and accepted practice in the legal profession to investigate claims and persons making claims in the product liability field, such as in the pending Corvair design cases," GM argued in its self-serving statement. "The investigation was limited only to Mr. Nader's qualifications, background, expertise, and association with such attorneys. It did not include any of the alleged harassment or intimidation recently reported in the press."

Even this denial of the worst, while admitting only what had to be admitted, proved to be something less than Boy Scout truthful. Intimidation of a witness before a congressional committee is a criminal offense, and GM's coy half-admission did not satisfy Senator Ribicoff. He scheduled a hearing to find out what had really happened, and the result was to make Ralph Nader a household word—to project the image on the nation's television screens of a lone young man doing battle like David against the Goliath of the corporate colossus. There were a lot of forgotten common men who could identify with such a champion of the underdog.

The admitted sequence (a lot was never formerly admitted) went like this:

Three days before Christmas, 1965, Eileen Murphy, who ran GM's law library in Detroit, telephoned the Washington law offices of Alvord and Alvord and talked to Richard Danner, a former FBI agent who was an attorney with the firm. She explained that GM wanted detectives to do an in-depth investigation of Ralph Nader.

Danner arranged to talk to Miss Murphy in person, and on January 11, 1966, she visited his office and furnished him with all the clippings and routine background information that GM had been able to accumulate on Nader. She emphasized, according to Danner, "that it was strongly believed by her and the legal department of GM that Mr. Nader was in some manner connected with or working for the plaintiff's attorneys in the Corvair negligence suits against General Motors, but that no compelling proof of this had been adduced as yet."

Danner was given the task of getting the "compelling proof," and the private eye he chose was Vincent Gillen, a barrel-chested former FBI agent who was now running his own detective agency in New York. Two days after Eileen Murphy's conference with Danner, Gillen flew to Washington and sat down across the desk from the attorney. A canny man with a love for modern investigative gadgets, Gillen had thoughtfully wired himself for sound, and as he talked to Danner, he quietly activated a pocket tape recorder. According to a transcript of this tape that he later furnished in Nader's damage suit against GM, the great motor firm wanted to find out a lot more about Nader than any possible connection he might have with suing lawyers. It wanted "dirt."

Here are some excerpts from the Gillen tape:

DANNER: Apparently he's in his early thirties and unmarried. . . . Interesting angle there. . . . They said, "Who is he laying? If it's girls, who are they? If not girls, maybe boys, who?" They want to know.

GILLEN: Wow, this is dynamite that might blow, Dick, you know that.

DANNER: Yeah, he seems to be a bit of a nut or some kind of screwball. . . . Well, they want to know, no matter what. . . . They want to get something, somewhere, on this guy to get him out of their hair, and to shut him up. . . .

On this very day when plans were being made in Washington to "shut him up," Ralph Nader was in Des Moines, Iowa, testifying at a hearing on traffic safety. He had been there since January 7, and by the thirteenth he was becoming worried. Nader, who feels that the full story about GM's snooping has never come out, had become aware of a strange man who seemed to shadow him everywhere he went in the Kirkwood Hotel. Once Nader encountered the man in the corridor outside his hotel room. At other times, the suspicious stranger just seemed to be loitering in the lobby when Nader was there. Nader began to get an "uneasy feeling" that Big Brother had an eye on him.

When he mentioned this to friends, they gave him peculiar looks. Such things might happen in Russia, of course—but in the free United States? Ralph had been working too hard, his friends thought. Perhaps he was becoming a bit paranoid.

By mid-February, this doubt about Nader's emotional status could no longer be raised. For Nader began to get feedback from friends, college professors, former legal associates; all were being questioned by investigators who said they wanted to learn everything they could about Ralph because he, lucky man, was being considered for a very important job. Some of those questioned, happy that Ralph appeared to be "making it" at last, telephoned their congratulations. The phony "cover" that Gillen had thought up for the GM investigation was slipping.

All of this was to be admitted eventually by GM. Other developments, like the bold advances of brunette and blond, never were admitted, but Nader insists they happened, and his track record for credibility is remarkably good. In addition to the advances, there were other incidents.

Nader was to testify before the Ribicoff committee on February 10, and he spent the ninth hard at work in his room preparing his testimony. But he was continually interrupted by annoying phone calls. "Mr. Nader, this is Pan American," a caller would say—and then hang up. Another said he was a Railway Express clerk, and would Mr. Nader please come and pick up a package? There was, of course, no package to pick up. Late at night, the calls became nastier, according to Nader, and finally one caller snarled: "Why don't you go back to Connecticut, buddy boy?"

Despite this harassment, Nader completed his statement and testified before Ribicoff's committee. As a result, on the following day, February 11, the "cover" of the Keystone Kops who had been put on his trail slipped completely. Nader went to the New Senate Office Building to get a transcript of his February 10 testimony, and two detectives, who had been staked out watching his roominghouse, followed him. They saw Nader press the "Up" button of the elevator, and they scurried up a flight of stairs to intercept him at the first floor. Unfortunately for them, Nader changed his mind, and when an elevator arrived, he pressed a "Down" button to go to the basement cafeteria. Having lost their quarry, the detectives charged about trying to relocate him. Their frantic hunt attracted the attention of a guard, who questioned them, took their names, and reported them to a lieutenant in charge of the guards. This officer, informed they were detectives who had been trailing Nader, told them to get out.

After the account of these devious maneuvers had been published in *The New York Times,* Senator Ribicoff notified GM that he was going to hold a public hearing into its conduct. With this announcement, the gored corporate monster began to thrash around in panicked spasms. What the devil was it to do?

Danner and Gillen were summoned to Detroit for conferences. Gillen denied that his agents had made the harassing telephone calls or tried to entrap Nader with girls, but he obviously expected his corporate employer to uphold his deep prying into Nader's private life and to abandon the pretense that all it had sought was information about Nader's possible link to the Corvair lawsuits.

Gillen expected too much, as events soon showed. GM notified Danner that it was not going to defend the investigation it had started, but was going to dump all responsibility for going too far on the heads of the investigators. When Gillen heard this, he blew up. He told Danner for the first time that he had tape-recorded the briefing in which he had been instructed to get enough on Nader to "shut him up"; and he advised Danner to "take an early plane to Detroit and in no uncertain terms to let the officials there know that I was not going to take the rap for the investigation."

In this atmosphere of every man for himself and the devil take the hindmost, the Ribicoff committee met in the high-ceilinged, ornate Senate Caucus Room on March 22. All of the television networks were there, with cameras trained on the principal actors in the drama.

Roche, the first witness, testified that as president of GM he held himself "fully responsible" for actions undertaken in the corporate name, even though "I did not know of the investigation when it was initiated and I did not approve of it." He insisted that the decision to dig into Nader's private life in an effort to "shut him up" had been made "by the people conducting the investigation"—in other words, by Danner and Gillen.

Senator Robert F. Kennedy (Democrat, New York) subjected Roche to the only really sharp questioning of the day and forced him to admit that the March 9 statement describing the investigation of Nader as a "routine" one had not been accurate. Kennedy demanded to know whether the investigation had not gone "far beyond what the original statement of General Motors indicated," and Roche replied, "I would say that is true; yes, sir."

When Nader took the stand, the contrast between corporate weaseling and crusading forthrightness was devastating. Nader denied that he had any connection with the Corvair lawsuits. His only interest, he said, had been to alert the public because the Corvair was an "inordinately dangerous" car. Then, in an eloquent passage, he denounced the kind of snooping to which GM had stooped:

"It is beneficial to explore the workings of such a routine investigation and its framework of operation. People all over should know that things like this go on so that they can, quite apart from laws, apply the customary social sanctions in a community which can operate to discourage or stifle such probings. But unless some definitions and sharpened values appear soon in our nation to limit such inquisitorial excesses, the employment of this essentially arbitrary power will continue its undermining of individual expression."

Then, in a final dramatic gesture, Nader drew a sharp contrast between himself and the highly salaried officials of GM. These fat cats of the executive suite had sneered that Nader was trying to make a personal fortune by sensationalizing the cause of auto safety, and Nader, in a display of pure motivation, made a striking pledge: he was going to devote all the royalties from his book to his fight for safer cars.

This was only the first time that Nader selflessly dedicated his private funds to public crusading causes. Royalties from *Unsafe at Any Speed* were considerable (60,000 sales in hardcover, 400,000 in paperback), but they were minute compared to Nader's windfall in his lawsuit against GM for invasion of privacy. That was settled out of court for $425,000. Expenses of the suit and his attorneys' one-third contingency fee ate up a huge chunk. Still, Nader was left with some $280,000, which he poured into the financing of his various crusades. He donates to the same causes virtually all of the money he draws down on the lecture circuit, an activity that often finds him making eight speeches a week at fees that range up to $3,000 a speech.

In a cynical age in which all too often corruption has become a way of life, Nader seems to many who have made the dollar their god just too pure-minded and dedicated to be real. In a world in which a common saying is that "every man has his price," many cannot believe that here is a man who cannot be bought. Robert F. Buckhorn, one of Nader's biographers, quotes a critic as charging that Nader deliberately cultivates "an image of himself as a cross between Abraham Lincoln and one of Christ's apostles." This skeptic sneers at Nader's living in a tacky Washington roominghouse; to him, it's just a bit of arrant showmanship. "Imagine a guy who collected $425,000 in a lawsuit from GM living in a place like that!" he says. "I'm not saying he should live in a penthouse, but a rooming house with a landlady who takes messages for him smacks of Madison Avenue image-making to me."

Yet all of the evidence seems to establish that Ralph Nader is exactly what he appears to be. All of GM's snooping produced nothing that was derogatory. "You and your family can be proud," Senator Ribicoff told Nader at the conclusion of the hearing. "They put you through the mill and didn't find a damn thing against you." In all the years since, though many of the powerful interests he has attacked have been waiting for Nader's halo to slip, this hasn't happened, and the unblemished Nader image has become so attractive that public opinion polls show many Americans would like Nader to run for President. This almost certainly will never happen, not only because the politicians wouldn't have him, but because Nader is too busy doing his thing. And his thing, his method, is to poke and pry and pressure the Establishment and its mammoth bureaucracies to correct injustices and to make the system work for the common good of all Americans.

The questions, then, arise: What produced so unique a man? How did he ever get going?

★

Nader was born in Winsted, Connecticut, on February 27, 1934. His father, Nadra, and his mother, Rose, had immigrated to the United States from Lebanon in 1925. They settled first in Danbury, but later moved to Winsted in the highlands of northeastern Connecticut, where

Nadra bought a ten-room white clapboard house and opened a restaurant he called the Highland Arms.

Nadra was not your ordinary restaurateur. He envisioned the Highland Arms as a place "where you feed the body and the mind." His daughter, Claire, later recalled: "You couldn't get out of Father's restaurant without talking to him, and the conversation was never about the weather."

A man passionately committed to issues, Nadra and his eldest son, Shafeek, haunted town meetings, arguing for everything from tax cuts to the establishment of a community college. This issue-oriented atmosphere carried over in the Nader home. The dinner table became the site for "think sessions," with Nadra posing a problem and all the children invited to take sides. Sometimes the debates became heated. "Even if you were hurt," Claire later recalled, "you were not allowed to run under fire; it was not appropriate to quit. You had to argue for the position you had, but the wonderful thing was that nothing said, no matter how heated, was allowed to disturb the family relationship."

It was a remarkable family atmosphere, and it produced, in addition to Ralph Nader, some remarkable children. Claire graduated from Smith College, took her Ph.D. at Columbia University, and became a social scientist at the Oak Ridge National Laboratories in Tennessee. Another daughter, Laura Nader Milleron, wife of Dr. Norman Milleron, a nuclear physicist, is herself a full professor of anthropology at the University of California in Berkeley.

Ralph Nader's most distinctive characteristics, his commitment to eighteen-hour workdays and his passion for hard facts, can be traced to this early environment. The 1930s were noted for their hard times, with the effects of the Great Depression lingering throughout the decade, and Nadra Nader worked long hours to keep his restaurant business going. The whole family pitched in to help. As soon as he was old enough, Ralph manned the cash register and developed the habit of talking to customers, learning their different viewpoints, picking their brains for information.

As a youngster, he played sandlot baseball incessantly and committed to memory whole major league rosters and batting averages. His height and wiry agility made him a natural basketball player, but even at this early age, his deeper allegiance was to things of the mind. His mother, Rose, who taught French, later recalled the day he came home lugging an armful of books. "What's this?" she asked. "Momma," Ralph told her, "that's the *Congressional Record* [the officially printed record of the debates in Congress]. I'm going to read them all."

A schoolboy who set himself the task of reading the entire *Congressional Record* naturally developed in later life into the man who gets his greatest pleasure, not from dates, not from socializing, but from spending long hours poring over statistical tomes to ferret out the details of complicated issues that need to be corrected.

From Winsted, Nader went to Princeton University, hitch-hiking his way back and forth to Connecticut. After Princeton it was Harvard Law School, then a brief stint in a Connecticut law office. Here he quickly found that the mundane business of drawing up wills and straightening out real estate transactions left him decidedly unfulfilled, and he began to look for a challenge. He found it finally in the cause of auto safety.

Nader had started thinking about the safety problem in 1956 when, as he says, he "saw a little girl almost decapitated in an accident when the glove compartment door flew open and became a guillotine for the child as she was thrown forward in a 15-mile-an-hour collision." Later, while he was at Harvard, a law school classmate, Frederick Hughes Condon, to whom *Unsafe at Any Speed* was to be dedicated, fell asleep at the steering wheel of his Plymouth station wagon. The car careened off a New Hampshire road, rolled over, and pinned Condon under it, half in the vehicle and half out. His spine was crushed, and he was condemned to a wheelchair for life.

The conventional wisdom before Nader—an attitude fostered by all the public relations skills of Detroit—blamed such tragedies entirely on the driver. The driver certainly was often at fault in such accidents. But, Nader wondered, was the driver totally to blame for the deaths and hideous injuries that resulted? Couldn't lives be saved if cars were designed to save them?

In the manner that was to become his hallmark, Nader began to read all the available literature and reports on traffic safety. He learned that 64,000 persons had been killed in auto accidents in 1964 alone. He learned that the automobile had cost *1.5 million lives* since the first fatality in 1899—more persons than had been killed in all our wars. He became convinced that seat belts, the elimination of protruding knobs and other interior hazards, and sturdier bumper and body designs could save countless lives. Taking up his cause like a crusader of old, he began to haunt legislative halls in Connecticut and Massachusetts, dunning his message into the ears of politicians during 1961–63.

Getting nowhere, shunted aside as a young crackpot, Nader went to Washington. There he became a consultant for Daniel Patrick Moynihan, then assistant secretary of labor, for whom Nader prepared a study of traffic problems and highway safety. The tome gathered bureaucratic dust but gave Nader the information on which to base *Unsafe at Any Speed*. His work for Moynihan and his book brought him to the attention of the Ribicoff committee, led to the confrontation with General Motors, and earned him instant national fame.

That was the beginning of something really new on the American scene, and the effect was quickly felt. Congress had been about to pass a weak traffic safety act, one that would have allowed Detroit all kinds of time to make changes and to produce, as Senator Ribicoff said, "fifty million new cars . . . free of any safety regulations." The backfire from GM's dogging of Nader changed all that.

The public and Congress itself seemed to agree with Senator Ribicoff when he said, "There is too much snooping going on in this country. People don't seem to believe that others have a right to privacy." The extent to which GM had gone in an attempt to blacken and silence Nader seemed to epitomize the insensitivity of huge corporate bureaucracies, and the average man identified with Nader. A shock wave of revulsion swept the original traffic bill into discard and led to the passage of the far tougher National Traffic and Motor Vehicle Safety Act of 1966. This act required the establishment of federal safety standards for all cars sold after January 31, 1968, and President Lyndon B. Johnson, in signing the measure, called it "landmark legislation." He added, "For the first time in our history we can mount a truly comprehensive attack on the rising toll of death and destruction on the nation's highways."

It was a remarkable triumph, the first of many for Nader.

His lawsuit against General Motors, as is the nature of such things, dragged on for several years, but when it was settled, Nader did what he had always planned to do: he used the funds to establish an organization that would keep exposing the flaws in the system on many fronts. He called this the Center for the Study of Responsive Law.

The center, which he eventually moved into a three-story nondescript building at 1156 Nineteenth Street N.W. in Washington, is a no-nonsense, all-work establishment. It has none of the graces of a large corporate or wealthy foundation headquarters, no ankle-deep carpets, no impressive mahogany desks and deep leather chairs. Characteristically, it is a jumble of cartons filled with raw research material, stacks of books and reports, and filing cases crammed with the sorted file folders of painstaking research.

Much of the basic digging is done by teams of students from the nation's elite colleges, young enthusiasts who have been tagged with the somewhat inappropriate nickname of Nader's Raiders. The "raider" term, suggesting as it does a swashbuckler about to charge the foe, is misleading because Nader insists on hard facts, and these can be obtained only by infinite, tedious poring over complicated records and careful, in-depth interviewing of personnel in the great bureaucracies that are being investigated. Nader himself is too busy chasing all around the nation to give personal direction to this research, a task he delegates to a supervisor selected for each special project. Even so, he is always popping in and out of his Washington headquarters, and it is his drive, energy, and enthusiasm that animate the entire effort.

His appeal to some of the most intelligent and best-motivated of the younger generation—to graduates from such institutions as Princeton and Harvard, for instance—is illustrated by the annual scramble of thousands to win prestigious summer jobs with Nader's Raiders. In 1970 Nader had 3,000 applicants for the 170 spots available on his summer projects. This appeal is all the more remarkable when one realizes that the eager young are vying for the privilege of working sixteen- to eighteen-hour days for practically nothing. Despite the fact that he pours into his operations virtually every cent he makes except for a $5,000 pittance for his own living expenses, Nader hasn't Rockefeller resources, and students on Raiders projects are usually paid only $200 for an entire summer's work, though in special hardship cases the fee may go to $1,000.

Critics of Nader—and, considering the powerful interests he has attacked, they are legion—have argued, hopefully, that he is bound to fall on his face because he cannot possibly keep control of his sprawling organizations. The time will inevitably come, they insist, when the research will be faulty—and one major blunder will discredit Nader. All that can be said is that nothing of the kind has happened yet. Nader seems to have an uncanny knack of picking the most capable and trustworthy candidates from the horde of applicants, and the research reports prepared by his Raiders have withstood every challenge and produced a host of reforms.

Typical was the impact of two of the Raiders' earliest reports dealing with the inadequacies of the Federal Trade Commission and the Interstate Commerce Commission. A long-recognized fault of federal regulatory agencies is that they tend to become the abject creatures of the wealthy and powerful business interests they are supposed to regulate. Lobbyists for the industries subvert agency personnel by granting special and expensive favors, and at times wooing a key executive with the promise of a highly paid job in industry after he has done his bit for the industry's cause as an official regulator. Nader's student activists documented the kind of dry rot and inertia that results.

Their sizzling report on the FTC charged that the agency was staffed with political hacks and incompetents, and had slumbered in a years-long siesta, doing almost nothing to protect consumers from shoddy merchandise and faulty practices. Officialdom reacted with disbelief. President Nixon, incredulous, asked the American Bar Association to investigate, and the ABA report, submitted in 1969, substantiated the charges. The FTC was so incompetent, such a do-nothing agency, the ABA committee declared, that it should be completely overhauled or abolished.

The report on the Interstate Commerce Commission charged that the agency had become the virtual handmaiden of the very rail, truck, barge, and household moving industries it was supposed to regulate. It accused the ICC of standing idly by while the railroads, in pursuit of greater freight-hauling profits, went systematically about the task of almost dismantling the nation's rail passenger system. The ICC, the Raiders said, was an "elephant's graveyard for political hacks," and its commissioners had been so ethically lax they had accepted delightful expense-paid vacation trips from the industries they were supposed to control. Again the report stirred the Washington official beehive. It triggered demands for a congressional investigation, and another presidential investigating commission concluded the Raiders were right—the ICC needed a thorough house-cleaning.

Other Nader task forces have kept up a drumfire of criticism on business and government bureaucracies that are so greedy and so insensitive that they represent threats to many sectors of American life. They have investigated pesticides in foods, the pollution of both water and air, the laxities of the medical profession, the abominable treatment of the aged in nursing homes, job hazards of all kinds, and the black lung disease and unsafe mines that cut short the lives of many miners in West Virginia.

As a result of these and other investigations, seven major pieces of legislation have been passed by Congress, and both the FTC and the Food and Drug Administration have undergone high-level purges. In addition to the National Traffic and Motor Vehicle Safety Act of 1966, which Nader personally influenced so greatly, his Raiders' reports have been largely responsible for a wholesome meat act, a national gas pipeline safety act, a wholesale poultry products act, a coal mine safety act, and an occupational health and safety act.

It is little wonder that such victories on behalf of common people have made Nader a hero to all kinds and classes of people. Consumers who want him to take up the cudgel for them deluge him with some ninety thousand letters a year. Tourists, when they spot him in the corridors of the Capitol, cluster around seeking his autograph, ignoring passing congressmen. His constituency includes little old ladies in sewing circles, gray-haired middle-class consumers, blue-collar workers, and even some wealthy business executives. Gordon Sherman, heir to the Midas Muffler fortune, was so impressed with Nader after meeting him that he donated $100,000 and pledged $200,000 more from the Midas Foundation to help the Center for the Study of Responsive Law. Sometimes, according to Ted Jacobs, Nader's former Princeton classmate who became his top aide in running the center, an unsolicited $10,000 check will come in the mail with the notation, "Here, spend this for your summer project."

Such has been Nader's impact. Fortunately, he is a shy and modest man who does not envision himself as some Napoleon of the consumer movement. He often expresses the hope that the young students, trained in research on his summer projects, will go out into their own communities and states and use the same methods in establishing their own watchdog organizations. He literally pleads for imitators.

"We want to encourage others," he says. "We want to start imitative efforts. If they must rely on me, then there is no future in the movement."

Again and again, Nader emphasizes his central theme—the responsibility of the individual, the necessity for the individual to act if the massive bureaucracies of the industrial age are to be brought under control and made to work for the welfare of all. "What we are trying to say is if you really want to make things better—take on the responsibility yourself," Nader declares.

Charles McCarry, in his *Citizen Nader*, sees the Nader movement as undergoing three stages of evolution. "Stage One," he writes, "was Nader, alone against the system; Stage Two was Nader and the Raiders, exposing sloth and venality. Stage Three . . . will see the development of models of social and political action that can be applied by anyone."

The spearhead of this final development has been the Public Interest Research Group (PIRG), staffed by a cadre of young lawyers who keep badgering the bureaucracy with investigations, petitions, briefs. The PIRG lawyers are not registered as lobbyists, and so cannot approach congressmen or senators directly. On the other hand, this status enables them to receive tax-exempt contributions, as lobbyists cannot, and there is nothing to bar them from harassing congressional staffs and regulatory agencies with their disclosures about things wrong and their demands for change.

Nader sees PIRG as the model for a nationwide activist movement. His field workers sparked enthusiastic responses on college campuses across the nation, and PIRG groups were soon formed in Minnesota, Oregon, Ohio, and Connecticut. One of the PIRG organizers, Donald Ross, saw the movement as presaging "a legal revolution." Where there had been in the past no more than fifty to one hundred public-interest groups are sprouting up like daisies across the country—a "thirty or forty *in each state*," and if that happens, he said, "the bomb that's going to explode when this takes effect will just be fantastic."

Important as Nader's own achievements are, perhaps his major contribution has been his unique ability to inspire others to go and do likewise. The *Los Angeles Times* said in 1970: "Nader has become, in four years, a national institution. He has brought about a near-revolution in U.S. law schools, and his influence is still sky-rocketing. New public-interest groups are sprouting up like daisies across the country—a few of them loosely connected with Nader, some of them inspired by him, and others copies."

These other public-interest lobbies range from John W. Gardner's Common Cause, with its 327,000 dues-paying members, to environmental groups and small state organizations. They have produced a sound effect like that of marching feet, and the U.S. House of

Representatives and Senate, responding to pressure, have undertaken some reforms. One that is particularly important opens to the public the so-called marking sessions at which bills are put in final form. Previously, such committee sessions were closed to both the public and the "people's lobbies," though lobbyists for special interests were often privileged to attend—and often took advantage of this opportunity to slip some last-minute joker into the legislation.

The new-style lobbyists for public causes operate on a very different plane from that of the traditional self-interest lobbyists. The new breed has no bulging corporate coffer from which to dispense expensive favors. It has to rely, as Nader does, on sound fundamental research, the assembling of an impressive array of facts—and the impact these make on public opinion, which, in turn, influences legislators.

Typical of the many battles waged by public-cause lobbyists was the struggle in the 1974 and 1975 congresses over coal strip mining. Strip miners in the past have literally torn the countryside apart, leaving gouged, scarred landscapes behind them after they have raped the surface coal veins of their rich bounty. When the Mideast Arab states precipitated an oil crisis in 1973–74, the United States became suddenly aware of the need for new energy sources, and agitation resulted in the increase of the year's yield from strip mining from 600 million tons of coal to 1.5 billion tons.

Environmentalists wanted Congress to adopt stringent regulations to compel strip miners to restore the land after they had ripped off the coal. Coal industry sources, naturally, wanted as few restraints as possible, arguing that costly environmental restoration would curb profits and discourage production.

The National Coal Association, with a $1 million budget, took out full-page newspaper advertisements, distributed pamphlets, and sent its lobbyists across the country speaking to business and civic groups. Opposing this industry lobby was the Environmental Policy Center in Washington. This is a low-budget conservation group led by Louise C. Dunlap, twenty-nine, and John McCormick, thirty-one, who rallied some associates from Friends of the Earth, an earlier environmental organization that had blocked appropriations for the SST supersonic airplane.

Miss Dunlap is a tough-minded young woman whose thorough grasp of ecology issues from the SST to strip mining has won the admiration of her lobbying adversaries. As she pointed out in one interview, her organization does not have the resources available to the mining industry and so has to rely on hard facts and a sharp focus on the central issue. The press, she said, "has helped greatly," but only after "they grill us severely on the issues" do they become convinced of the facts and reflect these in news stories.

Despite the heavy industry opposition, the environmentalists won their fight in the 1974 Congress, securing the passage of a surface mining and reclamation bill. President Gerald R. Ford vetoed the measure, but in early 1975 Miss Dunlap and Mr. McCormick returned to the attack. Congress again passed a strip-mining bill despite industry objections. "Louise and John have done one helluva job in representing the environmental interest," one industry spokesman conceded. The battle, however, was not yet over. President Ford again vetoed the measure, and the House of Representatives failed to override the veto by the narrow margin of three votes. The closeness of the vote encouraged the environmentalists, who vowed to make a third attempt to pass the strip-mining measure.

The strip-mining controversy was only one phase of a general campaign launched by business interests against costly environmental improvement measures. Senator Edmund S. Muskie (Democrat, Maine) expressed his belief in the spring of 1974 that "the current onslaught on environmental laws would have had more effect if it had not been for the public-interest lobbies."

Paul Duke, a veteran Washington correspondent, summed up ten years' experience on the Hill in these words: "Big money talks." In an analysis for the National Education Television network he pointed out that Washington lobbyists spent $6 million in 1973 in addition to all the millions ladled out to support favored candidates in political campaigns. He saw the emergence of the public-interest lobbies as "a good thing for Congress and the country." It was important, he felt, to have public-interest advocates like Ralph Nader and John Gardner matching the self-interest lobbyists blow for blow.

His comment seemed even more appropriate as the events of 1974 unfolded. It was a year that saw President Nixon forced to resign as scandal piled upon scandal. The Watergate bugging of the national Democratic headquarters during the presidential campaign of 1972, the huge $60 million slush fund contributed by powerful interests for the reelection of Nixon, the use of large sums from this cache to help "stonewall" the Watergate case, the dispensation of special favors to some heavy campaign contributors—all of these disclosures shocked the American public and focused attention on the manner in which powerful interests had purchased influence on the highest levels of government.

One of the more odoriferous deals, one that gouged every household in America, was a payoff to the dairy lobby. Dairymen began a drive in 1971 to get the U.S. Department of Agriculture to raise the guaranteed price paid to farmers for the raw milk used to make dairy products. Such an increase, it was obvious, would raise the price of every quart of milk bought by Americans, as well as the price of all dairy products such as cheese, and so initially Secretary of Agriculture Clifford Hardin rejected the dairymen's plea.

Less than two weeks later, he did a complete about-face, issuing an order on March 25, 1972, granting a 6 percent price increase. It was an action that, it was estimated, would cost American consumers at least $500 million a year. What was behind this somersault in official policy? How had the dairymen's private interest prevailed over the public interest in a time of rampant inflation?

The answer was to be found in a $1 million war chest raised by the dairy industry. Some $500,000 of this had been invested in the 1970 campaign to elect friendly congressmen and senators. But the real clincher as far as the Nixon administration was concerned was the $255,000 the dairymen pledged to the presidential reelection kitty.

A down payment of $35,000 was made on March 22, 1972, and the very next day Nixon invited sixteen dairy and farm representatives to the White House. William Powell, president of the Mid-America Dairymen, later wrote one of his members that "I sat in the Cabinet room of the White House, across the table from the President of the United States." He quoted Nixon as saying, "You people are my friends, and I appreciate it." Then Powell told his constituent: "Two days later an order came from the U.S. Department of Agriculture increasing the support price of milk . . . which added some $500 million to $700 million to dairy farmers' checks. We dairymen cannot afford to overlook this kind of benefit. Whether we like it or not, this is the way the system works."

Changing this "way the system works" became one of the principal 1974 objectives of Gardner's Common Cause. Gardner launched this "people's lobby" in 1970 with full-page newspaper advertisements and mailings asking the support of 2.5 million "concerned citizens."

Ironically, the $61,000 up-front money needed to finance this initial effort was donated by the Rockefeller family, their friends, and allied interests. A lobbyist's report that Gardner filed with the clerk of the Senate showed that the largest donation, $25,000, was made by John D. Rockefeller, III.

This financing enabled Common Cause to get off to a fast start, and by the fall of 1974 its 327,000 members were paying dues of fifteen dollars a year to help finance its activities. In a talk to Washington reporters in September, Gardner described the growth of his organization and some reactions to it. "I hardly had an enemy in the world while being concerned with such problems as poverty and racial prejudice as Secretary of Health, Education, and Welfare in the Johnson Administration," he said. But once Common Cause began to attack what Gardner called the "cozy arrangements" between vested interests and Washington officeholders, he became referred to on Capitol Hill as "that son of a bitch John Gardner."

Common Cause's major crusade of 1974 was not calculated to make Gardner better loved. Gardner's organization decided that the way to prevent more Watergates was to secure the passage of campaign reform laws so tough and so sweeping that private interests could not buy up the government. The testing ground chosen for this initial effort to change "the way the system works" was California, where Common Cause and its supporters got a referendum known as Proposition Nine placed on the ballot. This required:

★ Complete disclosure of all political contributions of fifty dollars or more, including the donor's name, address, occupation, and employer.
★ Setting of spending limits on statewide campaigns, with incumbents, who presumably would be better known, forced to spend 10 percent less than challengers.
★ Prohibiting lobbyists—this one really hurt—from spending more than ten dollars a month, including campaign contributions or gifts, to influence any state official.
★ Preventing state and local officials from voting on matters in which they have a personal financial interest.
★ Creating a Fair Political Practices Commission, which would have subpoena power and would hear complaints, investigate possible violations, and levy fines.

This sweeping reform measure, with provisions striking at the very heart of the moneyed interests that wielded such behind-the-scenes power in American government, triggered a donnybrook. Common Cause was supported by a citizens group called the People's Lobby, as well as the Sierra Club and the League of Women Voters. In bitter opposition were the California Chamber of Commerce, the powerful California AFL–CIO labor unions, major corporations, and practically every utility in the state. Even civil libertarians were divided on the issue, some wondering what effect the disclosure law might have on an employee who had the temerity to contribute to a candidate detested by his boss.

The most prominent politician to support Proposition Nine was Edmund G. Brown, Jr., who was later to be elected governor. So great was the popular revulsion from the Watergate disclosures that it became apparent, when the votes were counted, that Brown had picked the winning side. Seventy percent of the California electorate voting on the issue supported Common Cause's tough reform law. It was perhaps a healthy sign of the times, this adoption of a pilot model from changing "the way the system works" and making it more responsive to the needs of the average citizen and less the bought creature of high-priced lobbyists and their special interests.

It will take, of course, much more than the passage of one law in one state to effect such change. It will take persistent effort, and victory, if it comes, will not be easy. For the old-line lobbyists, despite scandals and Watergate, are at work as hard as ever at the old influence game—perhaps even harder.

A study by the respected *Congressional Quarterly* in Washington showed that in the first eight months of 1974 special-interest political committees had contributed about $13 million to congressional candidates and related campaign activities. This was $2 million more than such committees had spent in all of 1970, the last non-presidential election year. And the 527 business, labor, agriculture, and other specially registered lobbying groups still had $12.9 million left in their treasuries with which to finance further activities.

Singled out for special consideration by interests seeking special favors were members of the powerful House Ways and Means Committee, which writes the tax laws. Most members of this committee come from conservative districts and are solidly entrenched in office. Some faced no opposition at election time, and only four were considered even remotely in jeopardy. Yet by mid-September, 1974, fourteen members of the committee had received a total of $101,989 (some 20 percent of all the campaign funds they had raised) from just six major interests concerned with the provisions of the new tax bill they were considering. Even this figure doubtless underrepresents the situation because, despite the requirements of the new 1972 campaign financing law, a lot of political contributions were still being reported with just the name and address of the individual donor and no indication of what interest he might represent.

In such circumstances, what the record reveals may be only a hint of what goes on. Even so, it seemed significant that the three largest industry donors to the gentlemen of Ways and Means had easily identifiable selfish interests. First in generosity was the oil and gas industry; second, the real estate business; third, the securities industry. Oil-and-gas and real estate were lobbying hard to prevent the elimination of favored tax treatments they had been receiving. The securities industry was vitally concerned with two proposals that would lower taxes substantially for stock market investors, especially for those in the over-$100,000 income bracket.

The situation led to new investigations of the seamier side of lobbying. By early 1975 nine separate bills had been introduced in Congress calling for more stringent regulation of lobbying, and the Senate Committee on Government Operations, headed by Senator Abraham Ribicoff, had begun public hearings.

The last probe of lobbying in 1946 had resulted in the passage of an act requiring lobbyists to register, but the enforcement provisions had proven weak and ineffective. The General Accounting Office, the investigative arm of Congress, looked into the situation at Senator Ribicoff's request and found lobbyists ignoring the provisions of the registration act.

"The law as it presently operates is a disgrace," Senator Ribicoff said. "It prevents the American public from learning how lobbyists seek to influence the decisions of Congress and the rest of the Government. This secrecy must stop."

In hearings before Ribicoff's committee, senators Robert T. Stafford (Republican, Vermont) and Edward M. Kennedy (Democrat, Massachusetts) called the lobbying situation in the capital "a scandal and a national disgrace."

John Gardner, of Common Cause, pressed for stronger regulation and charged that most lobbying activity today goes on "behind a veil of secrecy." He said Common Cause had persuaded officials of the Federal Energy Administration to keep "contact logs" showing consultations with nongovernmental persons. There were 458 such meetings in five months, he testified—and only 6 percent involved such public-interest lobbies as consumer and environmental groups.

Washington was not the only capital concerned with the more questionable practices of lobbying. In Albany, the New York Assembly Committee on Ethics also held hearings. The new secretary of state, Mario Cuomo, had become concerned about the cocktail parties and dinners with which lobbyists wooed legislators, and he wanted all favors banned to dispel the "vast cynicism of that vast public about government." He urged adoption of an ironclad ban on all gifts to legislators. "Even that of a dollar ballpoint pen?" he was asked. Cuomo nodded. "Any gift at all," he said. It was a reply that recalled a bit of earthy wisdom contributed by pudgy Harry Gross, Brooklyn's multimillion-dollar bookmaker of the 1950s. Gross said a policeman became hooked and was on the road to being totally bought "when he accepts that first big black cigar."

Lobbyists have been offering inducements a lot more enticing than a big fat cigar, and the record shows they have often succeeded in exercising an inordinate influence on legislation. In 1966, for example, Congress passed what was widely billed as an income tax reform law, but when experts examined its provisions, they found that new special-interest loopholes had been written into it. One that was especially striking granted a depletion allowance similar to the oil depletion write-off for—yes, really—clam and oyster shells.

The average American has been for decades the unwitting victim of such self-interest lobbying. He needs comparably strong counter lobbies working for him if there is ever to be any hope of equalizing the treatment of different groups under the American system. The most encouraging sign today is that such lobbies are now functioning on a scale, and with a power and influence, never known before. Organizations like those headed by Nader and Gardner spearheaded the development, and their example has led to the proliferation of smaller but influential "people's lobbies." The movement has accomplished much in its relatively brief lifetime. It represents a force that, if it can continue to tap the wellsprings of American idealism and conscience, seems to hold out real prospects for better and more ethical government in the future.

BIBLIOGRAPHY

CHAPTER 1

McWilliams, Carey. "The Guy Who Gets Things Done." *The Nation.* July 9, 1949.
Samish, Arthur, and Thomas, Bob. *The Secret Boss of California.* New York: Crown Publishers, 1971.
Velie, Lester. "The Secret Boss of California." *Collier's.* Aug. 13 and 20, 1949.

CHAPTER 2

Bolling, Richard. *House Out of Order.* New York: E. P. Dutton & Co., 1966.
MacNeil, Neil. *Forge of Democracy: The House of Representatives.* New York: David McKay Co., 1963.
Marsh, Benjamin C. *Lobbyist for the People.* Washington, D.C.: Public Affairs Press, 1953.
Rienow, Robert, and Rienow, Leona Train. *Of Snuff, Sin and the Senate.* Chicago: Follet Publishing Company, 1965.
Schriftgiesser, Karl. *The Lobbyists.* Boston: Little, Brown & Co., 1951.
The Washington Lobby. 2nd ed. Washington, D.C.: Congressional Record Quarterly, 19 September, 1974.

CHAPTER 3

Bowers, Claude G. *The Tragic Era.* Boston: Houghton Mifflin Co., 1929 (hardcover), *The Robber Barons.* New York: Harcourt Brace & Co., 1934.
Josephson, Matthew. *The Politicos.* New York: Harcourt Brace & Co., 1938.
———. *The Robber Barons.* New York: Harcourt Brace & Co., 1934.
O'Connor, Richard. *Iron Wheels, Broken Men.* New York: G. P. Putnam Sons, 1973.
Sarnoff, Paul. *Russell Sage: The Money King.* New York: Ivan Obolensky, 1965.
Seitz, Don C. *Uncommon Americans.* Indianapolis: Bobbs-Merrill, 1925. Reprint edition, Havertown: R. West, 1973.
Thorp, Louisa Hall. *Three Saints—and a Sinner.* Boston: Little, Brown & Co., 1956.

CHAPTER 4

Elliott, Maud Howe. *Uncle Sam Ward and His Circle.* New York: The Macmillan Company, 1938.
Holbrook, Stewart H. *Dreamers of the American Dream.* New York: Doubleday & Co., 1957.
Thomas, Lately. *Sam Ward, "King of the Lobby."* Boston: Houghton Mifflin Co., 1965.

CHAPTER 5

Odegard, Peter H. *Pressure Politics: The Story of the Anti-Saloon League.* New York: Columbia University Press, 1928.

Taylor, Robert Lewis. *Vessel of Wrath: The Life and Times of Carry Nation*. New York: The New American Library, 1966.

Sunday News (New York), Sept. 1, 1974; *The New York Times*, Sept. 2, 1974. (For newspaper articles on the 1974 WCTU Convention.)

CHAPTER 6

Ernst, Harry W. "Behind the Handout Curtain." *The Nation*. March 17, 1962.

Koen, Ross Y. *The China Lobby in American Politics*. New York: Octagon Books, 1973.

O'Kearney, John. "Lobby of a Million Ghosts." *The Nation*, January 23, 1960.

Cook, Fred J. "Their Men in Washington." *The Nation*, March 30, 1964. (For a fuller account of the Fulbright committee hearings into foreign policy lobbying. The quotes used in both that article and this book are taken from the printed record of the Senate hearings.)

CHAPTER 7

Acton, Jay, and Le Mond, Alan. *Ralph Nader: A Man and a Movement*. New York: Warner Paperback Library, 1972.

Buckhorn, Robert F. *Nader: The People's Lawyer*. Englewood Cliffs, N.J.: Prentice-Hall, Inc., 1972.

Green, Mark J., et al. *Who Runs Congress?* New York: Bantam Books, 1972. (An analysis of the monetary pressures and hidden influences on Congress.)

McCarry, Charles. *Citizen Nader*. New York: Saturday Review Press, 1972.

Nader, Ralph, and Ross, Donald. *Action for a Change*. New York: Grossman Publishers, 1972.

Nader Study Group Reports. (Published by Grossman Publishers, New York, on various subjects.)

The New York Times, March 6, 1966. (The most important single newspaper article on Nader; an account of the manner in which he was hounded by General Motors. This was the story that caught the public eye and almost overnight made Nader a national figure. Other press accounts of Nader's activities are too numerous to mention.)

Transcript of National Educational Television program on public-cause lobbying, aired on Channel 13, New York City, April 24, 1974. (See also *The New York Times*, May 8, 1975.)

The Wall Street Journal, May 31 and June 6, 1974; *The Washington Post*, Sept. 19 and 20, 1974; *The New York Times*, June 6 and Nov. 3, 1974, April 20 and 23, 1975; New York *Sunday News*, March 9, 1975; *New York Post*, April 18, 23, and 25, 1975. (For some of the more important press and magazine articles on Common Cause, self-interest lobbying, and new investigations of lobbying.)

INDEX

Fred J. Cook has been a journalist for twenty-five years. He was with the *New York World-Telegram & Sun* for fifteen years, specializing in crime stories and interrelationships of crime and politics. He won the New York Newspaper Guild's Page One Award for best reporting or best magazine writing three times. In 1961 he received the distinguished Sidney Hillman Award for "Gambling, Inc." (in *The Nation*). Mr. Cook is the author of *American Political Bosses and Machines*, *The Warfare State*, *The FBI Nobody Knows*, and *The Corrupted Land*.